# ABOUT THE AUTHOR

Linda Williamson has worked as a medium for over twenty-five years. She gives private consultations, lectures and workshops, as well as taking services in Spiritualist churches. She has written four previous books, which include the bestselling *Contacting the Spirit World,* and has been interviewed many times by the media.

# BY THE SAME AUTHOR

# Finding the Spirit Within

*A medium shows the way*

LINDA WILLIAMSON

**RIDER**

LONDON • SYDNEY • AUCKLAND • JOHANNESBURG

1 3 5 7 9 10 8 6 4 2

First published in 2001 by Rider,
an imprint of Ebury Press, Random House,
20 Vauxhall Bridge Road, London SW1V 2SA

Random House Australia (Pty) Limited
20 Alfred Street, Milsons Point, Sydney,
New South Wales 2061, Australia

Random House New Zealand Limited
18 Poland Road, Glenfield,
Auckland 10, New Zealand

Random House South Africa (Pty) Limited
Endulini, 5A Jubilee Road,
Parktown 2193, South Africa

The Random House Group Limited Reg. No. 954009

Papers used by Rider are natural, recyclable products made
from wood grown in sustainable forests.

Printed and bound in Great Britain by
Cox & Wyman, Reading, Berks.

A CIP catalogue record for this book
is available from the British Library

ISBN 0-7126-0487-1

# Contents

To all my friends, seen and unseen,
and to all those who have helped
me in the compilation of this book

Love and light

# CHAPTER 1

# *Soul Stirrings*

It is said that we choose, before we come into the world, what our pathway in life is going to be. If that is true – and I firmly believe that it is – then I must have chosen to be a medium. I was born with the ability to tune into the spirit world. I didn't come from a religious family. I was never taught anything about life after death. Yet somehow I always knew that death was not the end and that those who had passed into that other existence were not in some distant heaven but around us all the time.

This knowledge coloured my earliest recollections. I was an only child and I spent many hours by myself, playing in the room that had been given to me as a playroom. But I never felt alone. There were always unseen people with me. I couldn't actually see them. I just knew they were there. Their presence wasn't intrusive or frightening. I accepted it as something natural. Sometimes they spoke to me in my head.

I never questioned who these people were. I knew that they had always been there and that, in some mysterious way, they belonged to me and I to them. They were closer to me than my own family, with whom I never quite felt I fitted in. Perhaps because of this feeling of alienation, I was a very quiet child. Often I would become lost in my thoughts and would hardly speak for days on end.

'I don't know what's wrong with that girl,' my mother would exclaim, exasperated.

I didn't tell her. Even if I had wanted to, I couldn't have explained this strange feeling. And I didn't breathe a word about my unseen friends. I was afraid people would think there was something odd about me. At that age I had no idea what a medium was. The word was never mentioned in our house, unless it was to laugh at some dotty old woman portrayed in a television comedy or to poke fun at Aunt Flo.

Flo, who was a relative by marriage, was the only spiritualist in the family. She was generally considered a bit 'touched' because she still spoke to Uncle Sid, who had died years before. This didn't strike me as at all unreasonable. She only visited us occasionally and each time I longed to ask about him but, under my mother's disapproving eye, I didn't dare to bring the subject up. I wished I could have sought her advice. She could have explained to me about my spirit friends and told me why I could sense them and no one else could. I could also have talked to her about the family ghosts.

There were two ghosts in the house. One was a tall, thin man, stooping slightly, dressed in an old-fashioned suit. He had a gaunt face and sad eyes. The other was an elderly lady with grey hair and a black dress that came down to the ground. How I knew what they looked like I couldn't have explained since I couldn't see them any more than I could see any of my other spirit friends. But I 'saw' inwardly, with an inner sense, which is how I see spirits today. Despite my mother's denial – 'I don't believe in ghosts,' she would say firmly – I think she sensed them too. My Uncle Harry, who lived with us, admitted that he sometimes felt someone in his room. We all heard the inexplicable thuds and the footsteps that creaked across the floorboards at night. Some nights there were loud noises from the dining room like someone trying to break in.

'Don't go down there by yourself,' my father would say, adding, as my mother set off, poker in hand, 'Take Harry with you.'

But when they got downstairs the noises would have ceased though the dog would be cowering in a corner and would rush upstairs, refusing to go back until it was light.

I was never afraid of the ghosts. I knew they wouldn't hurt me and I felt sorry for them. I tried to speak to them but I could never hear any reply. But I felt a response, as if they were grateful for my concern. In some way I couldn't define I knew the ghosts were different from the other spirit people around me. Their presence was heavier, depressing. Many years later, after I had learned that spirits sometimes become earth-bound, trapped in the places where they used to live, I sent out thoughts and prayers to them and asked my guides to take them into the light. They seemed to have done as I requested because after a while the presences faded away and I felt them no more.

When I was seven I had my first encounter with death. My mother's mother, who was bedridden, was living with us, being taken care of by my mother. One night she was taken ill and the doctor was called out to her. I heard the comings and goings from my own room and knew that something was wrong. The next morning my mother had to break the news to me that she had died.

'She's gone to be with Jesus,' my mother told me, which is what adults always tell children – and children always know that they don't believe it themselves. But she needn't have worried about how I would react. I knew my grandmother was there in the room with us. I could feel her smiling at me. Thereafter, my grandmother became one of those invisible presences that were so much part of my life. She brought me a feeling of comfort and happiness. I missed being able to talk to her and hearing her tell me stories but I was glad for her because I knew she was out of her pain.

Gradually, over the years, I became more and more aware of the spirits. Having kept silent for so long, one day, for some reason, I confided in a close friend at school. Her frightened reaction took me aback. She looked at me as if was mad. She must have told the other children, because I started to get some strange looks.

I was, however, very popular when one child brought in a Ouija board and several of us gathered in an empty classroom in the lunch hour to try it out. As soon as I put my finger on the glass it flew round in a most gratifying way, spelling out messages. We found that we could obtain information that was not known to whoever was operating the board. On one occasion, it told us where one of the class was going on holiday, something which she had told no one about. To our disappointment, our experiments were curtailed when the scripture teacher found out what we were doing and put a stop to it. I realise now how dangerous it can be to play with Ouija boards, which can invite mischievous or malicious entities. I had no idea then of the dangers and can only be grateful to my spirit friends for protecting me from harm.

By this time the voices in my head were becoming clearer. Until then they had never worried me but, because of my friend's reaction, for the first time I started to think that there might be something wrong with me. I wondered whether I was hallucinating. Then the voices began to tell me things I didn't know about. They were just trivial predictions about everyday events, but I could no longer dismiss them as imagination. I began to get worried. This was getting out of hand.

There was one place where I thought I might find help. On Saturdays I used to help out in the DIY shop my father owned. Wallpaper in those days came with a border along both edges that had to be trimmed off before it was sold. It was my job to put the rolls of paper into the machine and turn the handle. When there were no customers I used to stand at the door of the shop and gaze, fascinated, at the Spiritualist church next door, wondering what went on inside. Of course, it was closed on a Saturday and I never could get up the courage to return on a Sunday and attend a service. Even if I had, my family would no doubt have thought I was getting a bit 'touched', like Aunt Flo.

My only recourse was to go to the library, where I read every book on the supernatural I could find. One day a book on Spiritualism almost literally fell off the shelf into my hands. I devoured it eagerly, with a mixture of excitement and relief. This was the explanation I was looking for. Now I understood what had been happening to me over all those years. I wasn't mad or deluded. I was one of those curious creatures the book spoke about – a medium.

# GOING TO CHURCH

The startling discovery that I was a medium didn't immediately change my life. I really didn't know what to do with this strange ability. I thought about it a great deal and speculated about who the voices were, how they were able to speak to me, and what happens when we die. I also thought a lot about God and started trying to pray. Though I didn't realise this at the time, my soul was stirring within me, prompting me to begin my spiritual search.

I felt the need to attend a church and, the Spiritualist church being out of bounds, I took myself off to the Anglican church just down the road, to the surprise of my family, who thought that going to church for anything other than weddings or funerals was an eccentric thing to do. The church turned out to be what in Anglican terms is called a Low Church, evangelical in its persuasion, given to long sermons and earnest Bible study sessions. I didn't feel comfortable there. All that insistence on accepting Jesus into my life and becoming a True Believer made me nervous. I was afraid that I was going to be dragged off and saved whether I liked it or not. I couldn't have said with any certainty what I believed in, but the Low Church Anglicans' conviction that they alone had the truth and that the Bible was the literal, inspired word of God struck a false note with me, so I abandoned them for the High Church a bit further down the road.

This was better. The atmosphere was more tolerant. The music and ritual answered some need within me. I learned to play the organ and sang in the choir. Processing down the church felt strangely familiar. Though I had not heard of reincarnation, it awoke memories of a life I had lived as a nun, centuries before. Religion was very important to me in my teens. I sincerely sought to say my prayers and believe in Jesus. I was beginning to understand that I had a mission in life, though I didn't know what it might be.

I was confirmed into the Church of England. The bishop who performed the ceremony was Mervyn Stockwood, which pleased me as he had the reputation of being unconventional and sympathetic to mediums. But even while I dutifully took part in the services and recited the creed every week I knew deep down that this faith didn't give me what I was looking for. It offered no satisfactory answers to my questions such as why, if God is love, there is so much evil in the world. When I asked about life after death it was clear that on this Church too, had no information. I was told that I had to have faith. And no one understood about my spirits. If I tried to talk about them I received suspicious looks and there were veiled warnings about 'the devil and all his works'.

However, out of loyalty, I persevered with the Church for a number of years, through the rest of my school days and for some time afterwards, when I attended a secretarial college for a year. When I went out to work I even had a job for a while with the Church of England newspaper, the *Church Times*. On a couple of occasions, hoping that no one would see me, I sneaked off guiltily to a Spiritualist church, either the one that had fascinated me so much years before or one of the other churches in the area.

Compared to the church I was used to, they were plain and simple. There were no pews, just rows of wooden seats. Some had small altars with candles, others had just a raised platform at one end with a table and couple of chairs. The proceedings were conducted in ordinary light and there was nothing spooky about them. It was all very friendly and informal. All this seemed strange to me at first. I missed the dignity of the Anglican services and the pomp of the centuries-old ritual, though the extempore prayers were more relevant to the needs of the day. And I missed the choir. The singing was frequently painful, especially if there was no organ or piano to lead it.

Each service was presided over by a chairperson, who would begin by introducing the medium, a different person each week. The majority were women (which is why I have used the word 'she' when referring to mediums in this book), but there were a few men. After a hymn and a prayer there would be a reading from the Bible or some other spiritual book. The medium would then give an address, not a long sermon, often more of a chat about her own beliefs and experiences or some aspect of Spiritualist teaching. If she carried on for too long a warning glance from the chairperson and fidgeting among the congregation would signal to her that it was time to sit down. After another hymn, the medium would continue with the part of the service I had been waiting for, when she would single out members of the congregation and pass on 'messages' from people in spirit who were apparently around them. This, I learned, was called 'clairvoyance'.

I discovered that the standard of this performance varied tremendously from one medium to another. Many were vague and woolly. Nearly everyone seemed to have a 'little grey-haired old lady' with them. 'Could this be your grandmother, dear?' the medium would ask. And, on being told that the recipient's grandmother was still alive, she would say, 'Could it be your great-grandmother?' The 'messages' were similarly vague: 'I feel you've had a few problems recently but don't worry, things will be better soon.'

This was hardly encouraging. Other mediums, however, were in a different league. They spoke as though they were thoroughly in command of the situation and produced stunningly accurate descriptions and messages that obviously meant a great deal to those who received them. Though I sat hopefully in the front row I never received any particularly impressive messages, or none that sticks in my mind now.

But at least there I could talk about my spirits. Among these people it was perfectly acceptable to have such experiences. It was explained to me that mediumship often begins in childhood. Many children sense or see spirits. Some have invisible friends who may be spirit children. Usually the ability fades as the child grows up, and in time it is lost altogether. In my case, the fact that it had grown stronger over the years was apparently a sign that I had potential as a medium.

This made me quite pleased with myself and gave me a comforting feeling inside. I warmed to these kindly people and I liked what they told me about their beliefs. According to Spiritualism, everyone survives death and heaven is not reserved for Christians.

There is no sleeping in the tomb and no Day of Judgement when the righteous are saved and sinners are condemned to hell. When we die we simply leave behind the physical body and pass, in the spiritual body, into the spirit world. This world has many different planes or dimensions. The plane to which people go after death is determined not by what they believed and whether or not they went to church but by the kind of life they led on earth. What counts is living a good life, showing love and compassion to others.

These simple teachings, said to be based on communications from the spirit world, made far more sense to me than the Christian Church, with its exclusive creed and its threat of hell for non-believers. I felt at home in these little churches, in a way I had not done anywhere before. I wanted to delve more deeply into the philosophy of Spiritualism and to find out more about the gift of mediumship and how it worked.

When I was twenty-one my life underwent a complete change. I got married and, with my new husband, moved from London to Blackburn in Lancashire, where he had been offered a job. As soon as we were settled, the first thing I did was to locate the nearest Spiritualist church. I found it in a dingy street just off the main shopping centre. The next Sunday evening, I set off to walk there. But when I got near I hesitated. On one side of the road was the Anglican church, with its bells ringing out from the tall spire and lights shining through its stained-glass windows. The Spiritualist church on the opposite side of the road was small and unprepossessing. I felt torn between the two. The Anglican church stood for all that was familiar to me: the dignity, the music, the ceremonies hallowed by time. I would miss all that. But the Spiritualist church spoke to my heart. It offered a new understanding, a teaching I could fully accept and the chance to explore my gift. But while I stood and thought about all this, my spirits made up my mind for me. As if my feet were being moved, I felt myself drawn towards that simple church whose doors stood open in welcome. I was about to embark on my life's path.

## STARTING OUT IN SPIRITUALISM

The church I had entered was similar to the others I had been to before in London. As I attended the services week by week it became apparent that the mediums were of the same mixed calibre and the singing just as painful. But, as if to confirm that I had made the right decision, my relatives in the spirit world seemed to be making a special effort to come through to me. Nearly every time I went to church I received a message. My grandfather was one of the first to come. I was surprised when a medium mentioned 'a man called Harry who was a builder'. I had never known my grandfather – he had died before I was born – but, as I learned, it's not always the people we expect to hear from who come back to us.

But there were still many unanswered questions in my mind, so one day I made an appointment with the president of the church, a woman called Alice, and arranged to see her for a talk. We met one afternoon in the church and I gave her what must have seemed like a thorough grilling.

'How do mediums see?' I wanted to know. 'Is it like seeing people on earth?'

I was told that with some mediums it is, but many others sense rather than see. To my surprise, this was just the way I perceived people. In fact, it appeared that some mediums don't hear at all, they just 'know'.

'Why are the "messages" often so trivial?' was my next question. 'Surely, if the spirits are really there, they can find something more worthwhile to say?'

I was told that this is not always possible because of the difficulties of communication. A lot depends, too, upon the ability of the medium.

'Why do the spirits seldom give their names?'

A name, you would think, is the most obvious means of identification. But I was told that names are hard to convey, because of the way in which mediumship works. It is more difficult to get across something abstract than to convey a general impression or an emotion. This explanation I found hard to accept at the time. Later, when I began to develop my mediumship, I realised how true it was.

'What about seances?' I wanted to know. 'Do you ever hold seances at the church, sitting round the table in the dark, and, if so, can I come?' This was greeted with laughter. It seemed that seances were out of fashion. I was informed that 'physical' mediums, who could produce effects such as making tables turn, were in very short supply these days.

'Can anyone come back?' I wanted to know.

'Not necessarily,' she told me, adding, to my surprise, 'Some people in the spirit world don't know that it is possible to communicate. Others find it impossible to get through. Some are in an unenlightened state and don't even realise that they have "died"!'

I left feeling better informed – and aware that I had a great deal still to learn.

Shortly after that my father was taken ill. It was a long illness, during the course of which he had several stays in hospital and underwent a number of operations. I travelled down to London as often as I could. The last time I saw him he was in hospital again. I knew instinctively that he was dying even though all the family were trying to convince themselves, and him, that he would soon be home. I wanted to share with him what I was learning, to tell him that when the time came he would be met by someone he knew and would find himself in a new world, but I never had the chance to speak to him alone. Yet I think he knew this, in his own way. He wasn't a religious man but, as people are drawing near the end of their lives, they often seem to develop some instinctive sense of the world to come. It is as if awareness of the soul grows stronger as the body grows weaker.

As I stood up to go he reached out, weak though he was, and clasped my hand. 'Don't worry about me,' he whispered. 'I'm not afraid.'

A few nights later, after I had returned home, the call came from my mother to say that he had died. Of course, to me he hadn't gone far. He was around me in my home. Now that my mediumship was strengthening I was able to talk to him and I thought I heard him answer me, though I wasn't quite sure whether it was his voice or my imagination. When I returned to my mother's home I could feel him there as well. I even felt him present at his funeral, though no one would believe me when I told them so.

'You're imagining it,' was my mother's reaction.

I was hurt. I thought she would have been pleased to know that he was there. But the thought just seemed to disturb her.

I went back to the church, confident that it wouldn't be long before I heard from him, but to my disappointment this didn't happen straightaway. There were a few 'messages' that could have been him but they were too vague to be convincing. One of the mediums spoke of a 'father in spirit' but the description didn't fit. For the first time in my life, I felt doubts creeping in. Was he really there or was my mother right? Was I just imagining it because I wanted to believe it?

Gradually messages did start to come through, just a few sentences at a time, from mediums who did not know me and were unaware that I had suffered a bereavement. One of them described my father quite clearly, saying that he was very short (he was about my height and I am only 5 feet 1) and speaking of his sense of humour and his love of gardening. These were quite trivial facts, but to me they were important. These messages put my mind at rest, but in order to be absolutely sure I needed to receive more definite evidence, something that could only come from him. And for that I had to wait some time.

## DORIS STOKES

In 1974, my husband and I moved back to London. I wasn't sorry to go. I had never taken to Blackburn, which I found gloomy and depressing. We settled in Wimbledon, a suburb we both liked. Once again, as soon as I could I found the Spiritualist church.

It turned out to be a bigger and more active church than any of the others I had seen. It had a long history, having been founded before the First World War. Some of the most famous figures in Spiritualism had worked there, including Sir Arthur Conan Doyle, the creator of Sherlock Holmes and a leading protagonist for Spiritualism, and the celebrated medium of the Second World War period, Estelle Roberts, whose meetings in London's Albert Hall and elsewhere were attended by thousands of people. In keeping with that tradition, the Wimbledon church still attracted well-known mediums. One of them was a middle-aged, motherly person whose name was just then becoming known to the general public: Doris Stokes.

Doris was a remarkable woman, and the first medium to become a superstar. Her books were bestsellers and she travelled the world, appearing before thousands of people. I watched her rise to fame and admired the fact that she never let success go to her head. She remained the same ordinary, kindly person she had always been, which was why people identified with her and listened to her message.

I saw, too, the heavy toll that Doris's demanding schedule took on her health. In the last years of her life she was frequently unwell and had a number of cancer operations. But still she carried on, partly because of her determination not to fail the public, partly because of the huge publicity machine in which she had been caught up and from which she could not escape.

The stress obviously affected the quality of her mediumship. No medium works well under pressure. Towards the end of her life especially there were criticisms that the standard of Doris's work was disappointing, and she was accused of cheating by 'planting' people in the audience. I never saw any evidence of dishonesty. To me she came across as a humble, sincere person who could never quite believe the adulation in which she was held by so many.

Doris did a great deal to bring to the general public an understanding of Spiritualism and to dispel some of the myths and fears that surrounded it. Since she died, in 1987, a number of other mediums have sought to emulate her, but none has made the same impact or been taken to people's hearts in quite the same way.

## MY FIRST MEANINGFUL MESSAGE

During this time I was learning more and more about Spiritualism and I was often aware of my father's presence, but niggling doubts continued to trouble me. In the end, the confirmation I sought came from Ann, one of the mediums at Wimbledon church. Ann, who later became a close friend, was just starting her work at that time and hadn't given many private sittings before.

'I'm not sure if I'm going to get anything,' she began apologetically as we sat together in the church one evening after the service.

'Just try,' I encouraged her.

Ann began by describing my grandmother, saying that she had been unable to walk for the last years of her life. This was true – she had been bedridden for a considerable time. She then began to sense a different personality.

'I have the name of Alan,' she told me.

'That was my father's name,' I replied.

'He had an accent … American? No,' she corrected herself, 'Canadian.'

This was quite correct. Although he had lived in England for most of his life he had never lost his Canadian accent.

Then she said something very significant. 'He says that he understands now what you were trying to tell him when he was dying, and he wants you to know he wasn't afraid.'

For a moment I was too stunned to speak. Those were the very last words my father had spoken to me. Tears filled my eyes. I should have trusted my own inner senses and trusted him. He had been aware of my need and he had answered it.

I suppose that was when I became convinced of my vocation as a medium. I wanted to bring to other people the comfort I had received. But first, I had to develop this latent ability. And to do that I had to find what is called within Spiritualism a development circle, a group where mediums are trained. I sent out a thought to my spirit friends to help me, and before too long my prayer was answered.

# CHAPTER 2

# The Pathway Opens

One day at the church I was told that a development circle was being started, led by a medium called Kathy, and I was invited to join. I was very excited by this invitation. Now I was really on my way. I was hopeful that after a few months I would be taking services at the church and giving private sittings, like Doris Stokes and the other mediums I admired. Even if I had known then what a lengthy pathway lay ahead of me, how much patience and practice I would need before I got anywhere near achieving my goal, I would still have embarked on this path, because I wanted to be a medium more than I had wanted to do anything else in my whole life. But I wouldn't have been so cheerfully optimistic.

It comes as a surprise to many people to discover that mediumship is something that can be learned. I myself had assumed, when I started attending Spiritualist churches, that you either had the gift or you hadn't. This is to some extent true, in that there has to be some inborn potential. Some children exhibit this potential very strongly. Doris Stokes was one of these. She had spirit children as playmates who helped her with her homework. They were as real and solid to her as the members of her family, but she knew she couldn't tell anyone about them because she wouldn't be believed. Such a degree of ability is, however, rare. Most mediums, myself included, were aware of spirits when they were children but their mediumship ability had lain dormant until they started to train it – and this is what a development circle is for.

## LEARNING TO MEDITATE

The circle in which I sat met at the church once a week. There were five other members, all beginners like myself, although two of them were already working as spiritual healers. Kathy explained to us that before we could start to tune in to spirit we needed to learn how to meditate. Meditation is the key to developing mediumship. The senses have to be very finely attuned in order for the spirit communicators to get through, and this can only be done by stilling the outer mind.

I thought meditation would be easy. All I had to do was relax! In fact, it proved to be very difficult. As soon as I closed my eyes all sorts of thoughts flooded into my brain. Was I doing it right? What was I going to buy for dinner? Had I remembered to lock the back door? The situation wasn't helped by the fact that I was working as a temporary secretary at the time. Having to cope with a different job nearly every week was stressful and created a lot of tension in my mind that made it hard to relax.

Even when I did manage to relax a little I found that I was acutely sensitive to every movement and sound within the room. The sound of a chair creaking brought me back with a jolt. The noise of a car backfiring in the street outside had me almost leaping out of my chair! I was relieved that the other members of the group had the same problem. In fact, anyone who tries to meditate encounters this difficulty. The mental chatter, as meditators call it, that goes on in our minds all the time is not easy to silence. Our thoughts are like unruly children clamouring for attention.

But I persevered, not only in the circle but by putting aside a few minutes every day to meditate at home. I have to admit that for the first few weeks it was a chore. Early morning, which is supposed to be the best time to meditate, was impossible for me because I couldn't wake up. Last thing at night was equally useless because I feel asleep! So I chose the early evening, but even then I found it a struggle to tear myself away from the television and my comfortable armchair. Sometimes I wondered why I was bothering. It all seemed a waste of time.

But as the weeks passed it became easier. My mind was beginning to accept the discipline that I was imposing upon it. I had only to sit down in my usual chair at my usual time and my thoughts would automatically begin to wind down and I would feel calmer and more at peace. I never saw beautiful visions or received startling revelations, but something was happening. I felt closer to my spirit companions and I was finding an inner peace I had never experienced before. This helped me to cope with my everyday life. My mind was clearer and I was stronger, more confident. The stresses and strains of work became easier to deal with. My intuition was improving and I was learning to trust it.

Sometimes I would sink into a deep stillness. At these times, all the problems of life dropped away and I entered an altered state of consciousness. In this state, I was aware of myself as a spiritual being and knew with absolute certainty that there was something in me beyond mind and personality, something eternal that could never die.

Though I did not realise it at the time, in discovering how to reach this state I had discovered the most important lesson of meditation, which is to find that point of stillness within. When we do this, we get in touch with our higher selves, the innermost core of our being. Once we make contact with this centre, we have access to an unfailing source of wisdom and guidance. In the higher self are contained the memories of all our past lives. Our higher self knows why we came into this life and can direct us to the pathway we should take. It is our anchor, something solid to hold on to when everything around us in changing. The higher self is our divine spark, the centre where we are linked with God and are at one with Him. In the words of an Indian sage, 'Unseen but seeing, unheard but hearing, unperceived but perceiving, unknown but knowing … this is thy Self, the ruler within, the immortal.'

At that time, in the early 1970s, meditation was not as popular as it is now at the beginning of the new millennium. A number of my friends wondered what this weird new practice was I had taken up and thought I was going to rush off to India and join an ashram. I didn't have much in the way of books to guide me, so, apart from what I was taught in the circle, discovering how I could best reach this level of deep stillness, and hold on to it, was largely a matter of trial and error. Today there are numerous books available on how to meditate and I would recommend anyone who wishes to learn to study these. (I have included a couple in the Further Reading section at the back of this book.) All I will do here is to give a few hints, from my own experience, on how to meditate successfully.

## HINTS TO AID MEDITATION

Sit somewhere where you are not going to be disturbed. Make sure that the room is not too hot and not too cold. Wear clothing that is comfortable and does not restrict you. Have things around you that you find uplifting – beautiful pictures or flowers. You may find it helpful to have music playing in the background. There are many New Age meditation tapes. You might also like to try tapes that are programmed with subliminal messages to help you enter the meditative state. These can now be found in some general book and music stores as well as in New Age shops. (You can also get tapes to help you relax, give up smoking, or for a variety of other purposes.) The messages are not heard by the conscious mind but are picked up by the subconscious. This is a very power-ful and effective technique. Incense or aromatherapy oils can also be used to induce a state of meditation. Frankincense, traditionally associated with spirituality, is a good one to use. Rosewood blends well with this and aids in raising consciousness.

In order to get the most out of your meditation, it is important to practise regularly. If possible, meditate at the same time every day. You don't have to sit for long. Ten minutes is sufficient at first, building up to half an hour or more as you become more proficient. Quality is definitely better than quantity.

Always sit in the same place. This place will then build up a charge of energy which will help to uplift you. No particular posture is needed. The lotus posture (sitting cross-legged on the floor) is fine if you can manage it because it locks the spine in an upright position, but if, like me, you're too stiff for this, sit on a chair with your hands on your knees. An upright chair is best, as an armchair encourages sleep! Keep your back straight but without straining.

Before you can begin to still your thoughts you must start by relaxing both the body and the mind. The following is a well-known technique which I have found helpful. It is good to carry out this procedure at the beginning of every meditation or whenever you are doing any psychic work. In the beginning it may take at least a quarter of an hour to achieve a fully relaxed state, but with practice you will find you can reach the necessary depths in just a couple of minutes.

### PROGRESSIVE RELAXATION EXERCISE

Close your eyes and take a few deep breaths, breathing slowly in and out to a count of four. Focus on your breathing so that you are aware of nothing but the breath coming in and going out. Do this for about five minutes. Then bring your attention to your toes. Tense the muscles of your toes then relax them. Do the same to the muscles of your feet. Carry on slowly up the body: the hips, the abdomen, the ribcage and chest, the shoulders, arms and hands, the neck and all the muscles of the face. Tense and relax each part of the body in turn. Pay particular attention to the stomach, the shoulders and any part of the body where you hold tension.

When the body is comfortably relaxed, relax the mind. Let go of all the cares and worries of the day. Release all the thoughts that chase around in your brain. Continue your deep breathing. With each out-breath, feel a wave of deep relaxation, starting from your head and sweeping through your whole body, right down to your toes.

Then you are ready to start meditating. Before you do so, say a prayer for help and guidance. I always begin every meditation session with prayer as this helps to raise the consciousness. It is not important whether you pray to God, to Christ, to Buddha or simply to the Light, nor does it matter what words you use. The most heartfelt prayer can be wordless. What is important is your intention to dedicate your meditation to the highest light within yourself. When you have done this, you are ready to enter the stillness.

There are two popular misconceptions about meditation that should be mentioned here. The first is that meditation consists simply of allowing the mind to drift off into a daydream. This may be pleasantly relaxing but it achieves very little. True meditation is active rather than passive. It is a technique for focusing the attention on the inner self, what I call 'listening within', for the still, small voice that speaks in the depths of your own being. If you are meditating properly, at the end of the session you should feel energised, not sleepy.

The second misconception is that you have to make your mind blank. This is an almost impossible thing to achieve. Even experienced meditators can only manage it for a few seconds at a time. Instead of trying to do this, give your mind something of a spiritual nature to focus on. You might use a piece of music, a mandala or a picture. One of my favourite methods is to concentrate on a flower. Flowers, in their delicacy, make us aware of the wonder of creation. We all like to see them, but we take them for granted. How often do we really look at them and appreciate them? A little miracle of love and beauty is enfolded in each one. Try the following exercise:

FLOWER MEDITATION
Choose a flower that appeals to you and take it to your meditation room. Place it on a table in front of you, high enough to be able to gaze at it comfortably.

Sit upright in your chair. Keep the spine erect but without straining. Let your hands rest gently on your knees. Follow the Progressive Relaxation technique outlined above and say a prayer. Then fix your attention on the flower. Really study it, taking in every detail. Notice the shape and colour. Smell the perfume. Feel the softness of the petals and leaves. Hold your attention steady. Every time thoughts come into your mind, dismiss them gently and bring your focus back to the flower. Do this for ten or fifteen minutes or for as long as you feel you can do so without straining.

If you practise this exercise regularly, you will find that one day something remarkable will happen. You will feel yourself becoming at one with the flower, as though your consciousness is merging with it. And then will come that deep, utter stillness, that communion with the inner self, the God within.

## THE CHAKRAS

There are within the body a number of psychic centres called 'chakras', the Sanskrit word for wheel, since they appear like rotating vortices of light. A full discussion of this vast subject is outside the scope of this book, but there are a great many publications available which explain the system in detail. The chakras are situated along the spine, not in the physical body but in the spiritual body. Accounts differ as to how many there are, but it is generally agreed that there are seven main chakras, each one associated with an aspect of our psychological functioning.

| Name | Position | Function |
|---|---|---|
| Base | base of spine | grounding, survival, basic life energy |
| Sacral | just below navel | sexuality, creativity |
| Solar plexus | navel | will, sense of self |
| Heart | heart | love, compassion |
| Throat | throat | self-expression, communication |
| Third eye | between eyebrows | clairvoyance, psychic ability |
| Crown | top of head | spirituality, connection to the divine |

The chakras are the point of interface between the physical and the spiritual bodies. When you meditate or engage in any spiritual or psychic practices, you expand and develop. This leads to an increase in sensitivity. At the end of every meditation, or after doing psychic work of any kind, you should close down the centres and bring yourself back into your normal state of consciousness. This is a very important point and I will have more to say about it in a later chapter. But for now, I will just give this simple exercise.

### CLOSING DOWN EXERCISE
Picture a light above your head. Visualise it travelling down through the crown centre into the body. As it comes into the third eye centre between the eyebrows, see this centre closing like a flower. Take the light down through the throat, heart and the solar plexus. See it continuing to the sacral centre and on until it reaches the root centre at the base of the spine. Then see the light travelling down your legs and feet into the earth. Feel yourself grounded and centred. Visualise yourself surrounded from head to foot in an aura of golden light. Give thanks for the insights you have received then take a few deep breaths to bring yourself fully back into the physical body. Finally, earth yourself by doing something physical – walk about, stamp your feet, swing your arms, whatever you feel you need to do – or have something to eat or drink.

## DEVELOPING MEDIUMSHIP

As I continued attending the development circle I noticed the improvement my regular practice of meditation was bringing about in my mediumship. There was no sudden revelation as I had hoped. The spirits didn't suddenly start appearing to me. But the mental impressions I received were becoming clearer and the voices were stronger. Those invisible friends who had been with me all my life were still there. I now knew them to be my guides. They had been watching over me since I came into this world, waiting for the time when they could train me for the work I had come to do. I was very aware of my father as well. Although he would not have understood about mediums when he was alive, he understood now and he was giving me his support.

I also began to be aware of the spirits who came to communicate with other members in the group. This was something we practised week by week. After the prayer and the meditation period Kathy would ask each of us in turn to link in with spirit and see if we could 'pick up' a communicator belonging to someone else. I found that I could seldom actually see the communicator. I might get a hazy impression of height and build and know whether it was a man or a woman, but even this was more like sensing than seeing. It was more as if the spirit came very close to me, overshadowing me and giving me an impression of their personality. In this way, I was able to say something like, 'I have a very tall man here who had a good sense of humour. He died of a heart attack.'

Spirits often give the medium a sense of how they died. This is not because they are still suffering that pain – there is no pain in the spirit body – but because, as they come close in order to communicate, they recall the memory of their last days or moments.

Following on from my vague description, the person to whom I was speaking might say something like, 'That sounds as if it could be my grandfather.' I would then try to obtain something more from the spirit in order to confirm if this was the case. I might, for instance, hear him say, 'I loved my garden.' These words, however, would be heard in my mind, not outwardly. Alternatively, I might get a mental picture of a man in a garden. I would concentrate on what was coming through, trying to get more precise facts, something that would leave the person in no doubt as to the spirit's identity. This might be a more detailed description of his character, his hobbies and interests, or perhaps certain memories he and the person in the circle shared.

I would then receive whatever message the spirit wanted to pass on. Perhaps this would be something as simple as 'tell her I love her' or it could be advice or guidance. All the while this was coming through I would sense his emotional state – joy or excitement or, in a few cases, regret for something he had done in his life.

At least, that was how it was supposed to work. But I often went through periods when I couldn't get anything at all or when the impressions were so vague as to be worthless. During these periods I would despair of ever becoming a medium and would fervently wish I could give the whole thing up. Time and time again I would get ready to go to the circle with a sinking heart. As I walked along the road to the church I would be thinking, *This is a waste of time. I might just as well turn round and go back home.* But somehow my feet just kept walking towards the church.

And then I would have a good day when the messages came through strongly and I was filled with enthusiasm once more. It was an emotional roller-coaster but my experiences were similar to those of almost every aspiring medium. Development always comes in fits and starts and your resolve is frequently tested. But invariably, every time you feel discouraged, suddenly you take a big step forward and it all seems worthwhile again.

## HOW MEDIUMSHIP WORKS

Through all these setbacks and difficulties I was discovering how my mediumship worked and what I could do to help things along. This is what I now teach in groups and workshops, for I believe that if you understand the mechanics of something you are more likely to succeed.

Basically, spirit communication is all a matter of frequency. The spirits do not live in some far-off heaven. They are in a dimension not very far removed from ours which we call the spirit or astral world. This world actually overlaps with our own. The reason why we don't all see spirits is that the astral world vibrates at a higher frequency than the earth. Strange though it may be to think about it in this way, the spirits are around us all the time. Most of them are no more aware of us than we are of them.

Our ordinary five senses operate on the material plane. We only perceive things that are within the frequency range of our earthly dimension. In order to communicate with the astral plane, we have to use our inner senses. These senses can attune to higher frequencies. This is why meditation is the key to mediumship. Once we have learned to quieten our conscious mind our inner senses develop and the astral world then becomes within the range of our perception.

Sometimes our inner senses operate spontaneously, perhaps triggered by extreme emotion or grief. When grieving for someone you have lost you may get the feeling they are close to you. This is very common. Usually the awareness is only fleeting. For instance, you might catch a glimpse of the person out of the corner of your eye, but when you turn to look you cannot see them.

Mediums use their inner senses in a controlled, conscious way so that they can communicate with the spirits at will. The process of development is a gradual one, with the person's powers of perception slowly becoming heightened. There are no magic secrets. It is a matter of patience and constant practice. At first perceptions tend to be very vague and shadowy, and obviously fuzzy descriptions like 'I have an old man who used to love his garden' aren't enough in themselves. But this is the way in which the information starts to come through. What I learned to do was to concentrate on these impressions, as if focusing my mind with a fixed beam of concentration on the communicator. As I did this it was like a blurred picture coming into focus. Slowly the impressions became clearer and more accurate.

This learning process takes months or even years. Of course, the more natural ability you have to start with, the easier it is. And the more you practise and meditate, the more progress you will make. I always felt frustrated that it was all taking so long and wondered when I would ever be able to claim that I was a fully fledged medium. But you never stop learning. Even now I try to spend at least half an hour every day meditating in order to keep a strong link with the spirit world, but I am still frustrated by the fact that it is never as clear as I would wish.

The information mediums receive comes to them in a variety of ways. Clairvoyance, which is used as a general word for mediumship, literally means 'clear seeing'. Some mediums see outwardly, as if they were looking at the spirits with their physical eyes – though, in fact, it is their inner sense of sight they are using. They also see mental pictures. Clairaudience means 'clear hearing' and is the ability to hear spirit voices. These voices are nearly always heard internally rather than externally. They may be a thought impression rather than actual words. Language doesn't matter. If the spirit doesn't speak English, a medium will still pick up the sense of the words.

Mediums tend to rely more on one sense than another. Some see more than they hear, with some it is the other way round. I rely mainly on clairaudience. This was the faculty that was strongest with me as a child, and it has remained so. Although the voices are in my head, they are usually definite voices as opposed to thought impressions. I can tell, for instance, if the spirit is a man or a woman, and if he or she has an accent. However, I have worked to develop my clairvoyance and I see more now than when I started.

Clairsentience, or 'clear sensing', is the ability to feel or sense spirit. This is usually the first faculty to develop and is often initially no more than a vague impression, lacking the clarity of clairvoyance and clairaudience. But it can be developed to a high degree and there are mediums who never 'see' or 'hear' anything but just 'know' what the communicator is like and what he or she is trying to say. For me personally, and for most mediums, all three modes of perception work in conjunction. I see spirits, I hear what they are saying and at the same time I sense them. Sometimes, when a spirit draws very close to me, it is as if, for a brief period, I become that person, and this is when the communication is clearest and most accurate.

An important part of the training of a medium is the

development of the chakras. The most significant chakras as far as mediumship is concerned are the solar plexus, the throat and the third eye. As the psychic faculty unfolds, psychic energy increases and moves up the spine from the root chakra to the crown. As it reaches each centre the energy causes it to open and expand. The solar plexus centre, being the lowest of these three chakras, is the first one to develop. This is why, when people are sitting for development, clairsentience usually develops first. With the passage of time the two higher chakras, the throat and the third eye, also expand. The throat centre governs clairaudience. When this centre expands we begin to hear spirit voices. The third eye centre is called in Sanskrit 'ajna', meaning control. This is the main chakra of psychic activity and it governs the faculty of clairvoyance. When this chakra is fully functioning, all the psychic faculties come together and blend.

### CANDLE MEDITATION
This is a particularly good method for developing and improving mediumship.

Place a lighted candle on a table in front of you. It should be about 2 or 3 feet away from you and just below eye level so that you can look at it comfortably without straining. Quieten your mind by doing the Progressive Relaxation exercise (see page 25), then look steadily at the flame. Don't stare at it or strain your eyes. But you are allowed to blink! After a couple of minutes close your eyes and you will see the after-image of the flame as a white light inside your head. Keep your attention fixed on this for as long as you can. Whenever your feel your attention wandering just bring it back gently to the light. Don't try to do anything with the image, just watch. The light may appear to move upwards. It may change colour. Keep it in your inner vision for as long as you can. When it finally fades away, open your eyes and look at the candle again for another couple of minutes.

Then close your eyes and once again focus on the light in

your mind's eye until it fades. Look at the candle a third time. This time, when you close your eyes, try to hold the image in the centre of your vision. This is the third eye centre. When the light fades, continue to focus your attention on this centre and watch for any colours or pictures that arise. When these too have faded, bring yourself back to everyday consciousness by following the Closing Down exercise (see page 28).

This exercise, like the meditation on the flower, is very helpful for achieving that inner stillness which is so necessary for the development of any spiritual gifts. By stimulating the third eye centre you will increase your awareness of spirit. Practise this regularly and you may be surprised at the results!

CHAPTER 3

# *Learning About Spiritualism*

I sat in the development circle for several months. Eventually it closed down as some of the members had other commitments and could no longer attend. No one else in the group went on to become a medium but we all felt that we had benefited from our time together and that our spiritual awareness had deepened. After that I joined various other circles. Some of these were for the development of mediumship, others were meditation groups. I learned something different from each one and always enjoyed the peace and harmony of being with a group of like-minded people.

Meanwhile, I continued to attend the Wimbledon church.

## STARTING MY WORK WITHIN SPIRITUALISM

Although my attunement to spirit was improving all the time, I hadn't yet used my gift in public. The thought of standing up in a church in front of a crowd of people terrified me. Public speaking is, in any event, a nerve-racking ordeal. Mediums have the added difficulty that, unlike other speakers, they cannot prepare what they are going to say in advance, but have to rely upon their ability to relay the messages as they are received from the spirits.

Fortunately, Wimbledon church had an evening once a month called the Open Platform. This was an occasion when aspiring mediums and speakers could try out their abilities in front of an audience. It was designed principally for people like me, who were sitting in development circles, and was intended as a sort of half-way house between the undemanding environment of the circle and the more daunting task of conducting a public service.

The audience was composed mainly of regular members of the congregation who understood the difficulties of mediumship and were sympathetic. This made it easier, but it was still frightening to be confronted with a sea of expectant faces looking up at me when I had no idea what I was going to say. The first time I took the platform my knees were knocking. My mind went a complete blank and a whole colony of butterflies were fluttering around in my stomach. My guides seemed to have deserted me and I thought they had decided to take the night off.

With a great effort, I managed to calm myself by breathing deeply and praying that I might be used as a channel for anyone who wanted to communicate. Then I started to feel the familiar sense of loving presences around me and I was reassured that they were there after all. I felt drawn to a woman sitting in the front row and began speaking, describing a spirit I could sense with her, who I felt was her father. Fortunately, she was able to accept what I gave her and from then on the words flowed.

The Open Platform was of great value to me. I was able to gain confidence in a situation where, if I fell flat on my face (which I often did, figuratively speaking), kindly people would pick me up and encourage me to try again. The next step was to assist in church services, giving a short talk or a few minutes' clairvoyance, sharing the platform with a more experienced medium who did most of the work. Many mediums start out like this – it's a way of breaking them in gently.

One of my regular duties at the church was playing the organ, something I was very happy to do. One day the medium who was booked to take the service failed to turn up. Time passed and the congregation began to get restless. The lady who was to chair the service approached me hesitantly.

'I wonder,' she began, 'Do you think you could possibly ...'

'I don't feel ready for this,' I told her. I had never taken a whole service by myself.

'You'll be fine,' she assured me with, I suspect, more confidence than she really felt.

So I left my music on the organ (we had to sing unaccompanied that evening), grabbed another student medium, Ann, who had given me the message from my father a while before, and took her up on to the platform with me.

The church at Wimbledon is a big one. That night it seemed to have miraculously grown. The organ at the far end seemed a mile away and the space between was filled with strangers, some of whom did not look very approachable. But there were some faces I recognised, giving us smiles of encouragement. As the strains of the first hymn died away I sent a frantic prayer 'upstairs', as I had taken to calling my guides, and began.

I would like to say that the evening was a brilliant success. Actually, we struggled through. Some of the spirits I described were recognised and their messages acknowledged, but every time someone said 'no' I felt like crawling under the chair with embarrassment. However, it was a beginning. After this I progressed to taking services at other churches.

One valuable lesson I learned during this time was trust – trust in my guides and the information they were giving me. It takes courage, even in the context of a Spiritualist church service, to address a complete stranger and pass on some message from a person who has died – and hope that they are going to accept it. No medium can be accurate all the time. Because of the nature of spirit communication, there are bound to be times when things get distorted or don't come through clearly. For this reason, I will never insist that I am always right. But I know that, when I hear those quiet spirit voices speaking in my mind, what they say is always correct, however unlikely or incomprehensible the message may sound. My job is not to question or interpret but merely to pass the message on.

The amount of information the spirits can convey during these short demonstrations of clairvoyance is very limited. And if the medium is working under difficult conditions, so are the spirits. They must try to express themselves in just a few words to each person, and they must wonder sometimes what they can say that will be relevant and meaningful. If you think of a crowd of people, all clamouring to get through at the same time, on a limited number of telephone lines and all those lines faint and crackly, you will have some idea of what it is like. The remarkable thing is that anything gets through at all!

In travelling round the churches I soon found that all of them had one of two members of the congregation who made my job harder. Mediums, being so sensitive, especially those who are inexperienced, are very vulnerable to any unfavourable reaction they receive from the recipients of the messages. I dreaded the people who said 'no' to everything as a matter of principle – and who would often come up to me when the service was over and admit that what I said was true. 'You were right,' one such woman confessed. 'That was definitely my mother. But I never got on with her so I wasn't going to accept her.'

Almost as bad were the 'message-grabbers' who fixed me with an intense stare, willing me to speak to them and, if I didn't, would put up their hands, claiming that someone else's father or grand-mother belonged to them.

I met many kind and lovely people whose warmth and friendship gave me great encouragement, but I also came across some curious eccentrics. There was the woman who was convinced that she was the reincarnation of the Virgin Mary, and the man who had a hot line to Jesus. Then there was the church president who was afraid to be left alone in his own church at night in case he saw a ghost. One old man refused to put a donation in the collection box unless he had received a message. My favourite was the elderly couple who brought their sandwiches with them to the midweek service and sat in the front row, happily munching away during the clairvoyance.

Surprising though it may seem, I never witnessed any ghostly apparitions in any church I went to, nor were the congregation disturbed by raps on the walls or by the furniture levitating. On one occasion a loud and inexplicable rap from the back of the church gave the medium who was taking the service such a fright that he assured the congregation if it happened again he would be straight out the door! The only supernatural noises I ever heard came after an elderly member of the congregation died and his ashes, which were due to be scattered in the garden of remembrance behind the church, were left for a time in a cupboard in the healing sanctuary. Every time the sanctuary was used, faint taps would be heard coming from inside the cupboard. No one was too perturbed by this. 'We must get around to scattering those ashes sometime,' the president remarked – and promptly forgot about it until the next hint from the deceased. When eventually the ashes were scattered, the noises ceased.

## SPIRITUALISM – YESTERDAY AND TODAY

Despite the growing interest in mediumship today, Spiritualism as a movement is not very well understood, even among New Age thinkers. So this might be a good point at which to explain something of its history and development and how the movement is organised today.

Although communication with the spirit world has existed since earliest times, the modern Spiritualist movement started in America with two sisters, Kate and Margaret Fox. In 1848 the Fox sisters moved with their parents into a farmhouse in Hydesville, New York State. The house already had the reputation of being haunted, and before they had been there many months poltergeist activity broke out. Initially the sisters were frightened when the ghost rapped on the walls of their bedroom and made the beds shake. Then one of them challenged the ghost by clapping her hands several times and inviting it to reply. The ghost responded by rapping the same number of times. Nervous but intrigued, their mother invited the neighbours in to listen.

One of the neighbours had the idea of refining the method of communication by calling over the letters of the alphabet and asking the ghost to rap when the appropriate letter was reached.

In this way they established that the ghost was that of a pedlar who had been murdered in the house by a previous tenant and his body buried in the cellar. Some of the men dug up the cellar floor but they had to stop when they came to water. However, fifty years later some children playing in the cellar discovered a skeleton and, buried beside it, a pedlar's tin box.

The Hydesville incident occurred at a time when there was a great interest in the supernatural all over America. Perhaps for this reason it generated enormous publicity and helped to inspire a craze for spirit rapping. This craze spread like wildfire throughout the continent and from there to Britain and Europe. The Fox sisters became the first professional mediums, and for the next forty years they toured America giving seances. Their careers ended ignominiously in accusations of fraud but by this time the Spiritualist movement was firmly established, with churches and centres in every town.

The new movement was scorned by sceptics and denounced by the Church. Spiritualists were severely persecuted. They were driven out of their homes and their jobs. Stones were thrown at them in the street. Despite this, or perhaps because of it, Spiritualism flourished. For its supporters, it provided something that had never been known before in the history of mankind – a means of communicating with loved ones who had died, and certain proof of life after death.

The late nineteenth century was the heyday of Spiritualism. The most bizarre and extraordinary phenomena were reported. In Victorian Britain, the exploits of mediums were unlike anything seen today. In dark seance rooms, trumpets flew around, chairs and tables – and mediums – levitated, musical instruments played by themselves. Most amazing of all were the materialisation seances, at which spirits appeared in solid form.

Many accounts of these seances were no doubt highly coloured. There was a great deal of fraud. On far too many occasions sceptical sitters would grab hold of a materialised 'spirit' only to find themselves clutching the medium herself, wrapped in a sheet.

But some of the phenomena were genuine, reported by sober and reliable witnesses. Scientists and academics were generally dismissive of these reports, but in England in 1882 a group of Cambridge academics formed the Society for Psychical Research to investigate the subject.

The Society compiled thousands of cases, all meticulously recorded. They investigated mediums carefully, putting them under close scrutiny and requiring them to work under strictly controlled conditions then assessing the evidence they produced. The results were mixed. Some mediums appeared to be capable of astonishing feats, but the investigators were often disappointed when a medium in whom they had high hopes turned out to be a fraud. The evidence was hotly argued and soon the Society split into two factions, the believers and the sceptics, with the sceptics being in the majority.

As time passed the style of mediumship changed. The so-called 'physical' mediumship which produced the dramatic, physical type of phenomena was replaced by what is called 'mental' mediumship, in which the medium goes into a trance and the spirits speak through her. This type of mediumship was less easy to fake. The spirits gave information about themselves which could be verified. A number of excellent mediums, such as Mrs Piper, Mrs Leonard and Eileen Garrett, whose integrity was never questioned, submitted themselves for investigation by the Society. The evidence they provided is some of the most convincing ever given for life after death and is still studied by researchers today. In time trance mediumship became less common and was replaced by the style of mediumship that is general today, where the medium is fully conscious and aware of what is coming through her.

Spiritualism enjoyed a great increase in popularity during both world wars, with so many people desperate to contact loved ones who had died. Many dedicated mediums toiled to fulfil that need. The years during and after the First World War produced some of the best mediums of all time, such as Estelle Roberts, Helen Hughes, Bertha Harris and Ena Twigg.

But Spiritualism had no legal standing and mediums were still liable to prosecution. In 1944 Helen Duncan was charged under the antiquated Witchcraft Act and sentenced to nine months' imprisonment. The trial at the Old Bailey was a sensation. It was suspected at the time, and has since been proved, that Mrs Duncan was targeted by the authorities because she had received communications from servicemen who described where and how they had died and, in doing so, had divulged classified information that had been withheld from the public. The authorities were afraid that she might give away the secrets of the D-Day landings that were then being planned, and so were determined to silence her.

Though her trial was considered by many a great miscarriage of justice, it did have one good result as far as Spiritualism was concerned. In 1951 the Witchcraft Act was repealed and replaced by the Fraudulent Mediums Act. Spiritualists regarded this as a great step forward, claiming that by speaking of fraudulent mediums, the act implied that there was such a thing as genuine communication from the spirit world.

Since the end of the Second World War Spiritualism has declined, affected, among other things, by the general decline in church attendance. Nevertheless, it does still have a considerable following. There are Spiritualist movements in America, Canada, Australia and many other parts of the world. In Europe, although there are no churches, there are many Spiritualist groups and the subject is attracting increasing interest. The International Spiritualist Federation, which exists to bring Spiritualists of all nationalities together, has a worldwide membership and holds international conferences.

## SPIRITUALIST CHURCHES

There are hundreds of Spiritualist churches throughout Britain. All of these offer religious services, demonstrations of clairvoyance and healing. From time to time they also put on workshops, lectures and other events. Development circles like the one in which I sat are sometimes available. Each church is run by a president and committee, all unpaid volunteers. Some churches are poorly attended; others, where there is an enthusiastic committee, are flourishing. While some churches have their own building others are so-called 'suitcase churches' and hire a hall in a community centre or somewhere similar.

I have taken services in Quaker meeting houses, converted cellars and scout huts. There was one church that met in a room above a bar, the ethereal spirits mingling with the more worldly spirits in the bar below. But though the premises may leave a lot to be desired, a great deal of love goes into the running of these little churches. The committee turn up some time before the service is due to start in order to put out chairs, arrange flowers and lay a cloth over a table to turn it into a makeshift altar. By the time the congregation arrives, a cold, draughty room has been transformed into a chapel.

The mediums who serve Spiritualist churches often travel many miles to do so. Churches try to arrange that no medium should serve the church more than three or four times a year. This is because, if the medium gets to know the regular members of the congregation too well, the messages she gives may be unconsciously coloured by her knowledge of them, their lives and their families. For this reason, like most mediums, I prefer to work with strangers rather than people I know well.

This travelling can be very rewarding. I enjoy visiting new churches and making new friends. But it does have its down side. It can be very time consuming. My pet hate is driving to a town I don't know, getting lost in the one-way system and arriving at the church breathless with only two minutes to go before the start of the service!

Some churches are easier to work in than others. It depends upon the committee running it and the congregation. When there is sincerity and harmony in the church a good energy will be created in which the spirit communication flows easily. But, human nature being what it is, harmony does not always prevail and from time to time disputes and squabbles arise.

I arrived at one church to be greeted by the secretary with the words, 'We've just had a blazing row on the committee.' When I walked into the building you could have cut the air with a knife. Needless to say, the service didn't go very well. I must add, however, that this is unusual. In general, Spiritualist churches have a warm, friendly atmosphere.

Giving a demonstration of clairvoyance is not as nerve-racking for me now as it was when I started. I always encourage aspiring mediums by telling them that the first twenty-five years are the worst – after that, you get used to it. However, each service is a fresh challenge and I am constantly aware of my responsibility both to the spirit world and to those seated in front of me.

Before I stand up to begin the service I attune to 'upstairs' and make my mind as open and receptive as I can. As I do this, I have a sense of numerous spirits gathering around me, each wishing to communicate with someone within the congregation. The guides sort them out for me, deciding who should be given the opportunity to come forward. I like to picture them lining up the hopeful applicants in an orderly queue!

Usually I feel drawn to a particular person within the congregation and I know that the guides want me to speak to him. I then start by describing any spirits I can feel with him, whether I see these spirits, sense them or hear them speaking to me. At other times I am aware of the communicator first but don't know who he or she belongs to. Again, I start by describing the spirit person and giving as much information as I can, in the hope that someone will be able to identify him or her. Sometimes no one does, either because I have got it wrong or because the person to whom the spirit belongs is too shy to speak up in public. But usually someone will put up a hand and say, 'I know who that is'; if not, I will be directed by my guides to the appropriate person.

## MESSAGES

Spirit messages play a very significant part in Spiritualism, but they are often derided as trivial and mundane. They may indeed seem so to outsiders, who wonder if the spirits have nothing better to do than engage in idle chat, and this was in fact my thought when I first started attending Spiritualist churches. But to dismiss them so summarily is to misunderstand the nature of this kind of spirit communication. Though there may be communications from guides giving spiritual direction, in the main the purpose of clairvoyance is to give spirits the opportunity to get in contact with their loved ones on earth. These spirits are not highly evolved beings coming from angelic realms. They are ordinary men and women who are still involved with those they have left behind on earth. They are concerned with their families' joys and pains, their problems and whatever is going on in their lives, so that is what they talk about.

I was stunned when I first received messages from relatives, some of whom I had never met but who obviously knew a great deal about me. Even if I had not already known inwardly that I had spirit companions with me, I'm sure that in time I would have realised this from what I was told, and would have been sufficiently convinced to investigate further.

For a person who comes into a church desperate to make contact with someone who has died, messages may give much needed reassurance and evidence that there is a life beyond. For regular church attenders, the continued contact with loved ones is a source of comfort. Unfortunately, the standard of mediumship in churches today falls far short of what it should be and messages are often so vague as to be completely unconvincing. Because of this, newcomers are sometimes disappointed. But when the medium is good, even a few short words can be deeply significant to the recipient – though no doubt trivial to anyone else present. I have often seen people burst into tears of joy upon receiving a communication from someone they loved. This can literally change the person's life, bringing new hope. It is these occasions, when I am able to bring this sort of comfort to a person who perhaps is grieving after a recent bereavement, that make my work so satisfying and worthwhile.

The spirits often speak of how they have changed since entering the spirit world, how they have come to understand spiritual values and now see their earthly life in a different perspective. But despite this they are still basically the same people they were when they were on earth, retaining many of their previous characteristics, interests and mannerisms. It is these things that make them recognisable to those who knew them.

I try to be tactful when I pass on information, expressing anything very personal or confidential in a way that will be understood by the recipient and no one else. But if the spirit was a blunt, outspoken person when he was alive, he is likely to be just as blunt and outspoken in his messages. And as I am just the messenger and simply relay what I am given, I sometimes don't realise the import of what I am saying, and this occasionally causes me embarrassment.

One man came through to a woman in the congregation, Jean, complaining that his daughter-in-law had neglected him. He was aggrieved at this, and although he admitted that he had upset her and now wanted to make his peace, he couldn't resist making some barbed comments about her attitude to him. I repeated these with some misgivings, asking the woman, 'Do you feel you can pass this on to his daughter-in-law?' 'I am his daughter-in-law,' she replied. True to form, he had come to apologise but had still managed to annoy her!

## THE BELIEFS OF SPIRITUALISM

But the messages are not the whole of Spiritualism. It also has a philosophy based upon the information given, through mediums, by spirit teachers. This philosophy contains no elaborate creeds. To me it is reasonable and plausible and far more acceptable than the teachings of the Christian Church. It answers many of the questions to which the Church could never provide me with satisfactory answers.

First and foremost, Spiritualism solves the mystery of what happens after death. It states that death is merely a transition to a higher plane of consciousness. When people die they cast off their physical body and enter the spirit or astral world, where they are met by loved ones. The astral world has many different planes or dimensions. The spirits gradually progress through these dimensions, rising ever and ever higher as their consciousness expands. This process may take hundreds or even thousands of years in earth time, though they live in a timeless state. As part of their progression they may return to earth for other lives. (Reincarnation is a contentious issue among Spiritualists, though most now accept it.) But after each life we go back to the spirit world, which is our true home. Our eventual destiny is to reach the ultimate state of union with God, the great Creator of all. This is the state of cosmic consciousness and could, in Christian terms, be described as heaven.

Spiritualism offers a solution to the age-old problem of evil. God created us with freewill and gave us the choice between good and evil. This struggle, which goes on through countless lifetimes, is a part of the learning process. It is only by experiencing both that we can develop our inner light. The law of karma (of which more later) ensures that there is justice. We pay for our sins and receive reward for our virtues.

Although there is no final Day of Judgement, with God admitting saints to heaven and consigning sinners to eternal damnation, spirits have to review their lives and face up to whatever they have done wrong. This is a self-judgement and it can be a painful process because they are made aware of the suffering they have caused to others and the harm that has resulted from their actions.

A person who had led a life of cruelty and evil, closing his heart to pity, would descend to the hell regions of the astral plane where he would be with others of his kind, and here he would pay the price of his crimes. For instance, a war criminal who had been responsible for the death of hundreds of people would have to confront all his victims and feel within himself the agony he had caused them. This would be his self-inflicted punishment. The darkness in his soul would hold him imprisoned in this region, which is not one of fire and brimstone but is cold and desolate. However, he need not be condemned for ever. As soon as he was ready to reform he would be helped to cleanse himself and to begin the long ascent upwards into the light.

On the other hand, someone whose life had been devoted to love and compassion would rise at once to the higher planes, drawn there by the goodness within their hearts. Someone like Mother Teresa, for instance, would no doubt soar straight into the angelic regions, to be received with great rejoicing. Most people are neither great saints nor great sinners. For them, a beautiful world awaits, a world full of opportunities to learn and progress and from which they can, if they wish, keep in touch with those on earth.

At the heart of Spiritualism is the ideal of love and service to others. This ideal runs through the teaching of all the guides and in fact lies at the heart of all religions. We are in this world to develop the spark of divinity which is within each one of us, our higher self. When we do this we join in our consciousness with the holy angels and teachers who watch over humankind. We become co-workers with them in the task of bringing the light of spirit to all humanity.

Every Spiritualist church service includes, as well as the demonstration of clairvoyance, an address by the medium on some aspect of Spiritualist belief and philosophy. This is to me the most important part of the service and the part I most enjoy doing. It gives me the opportunity to share something of what I have learned through the years, both from my own guides and from the many wise beings on earth and in the spirit world, whose teachings help us to make sense of our existence. Of course, like everyone, I never stop learning and the more I learn the more I am awestruck by the wonder of the spiritual universe and the loving care in which we and all the world are held.

My function in taking a service, as I see it, is to provide a channel of communication for the spirit world to use in whatever way it sees fit, both in the individual communications from spirit loved ones and in the teaching. There are, it has to be admitted, many among the congregations whose interest does not extend beyond the messages. But the majority of Spiritualists understand that they are there not only to receive, but also to give. The love and prayer and the distant healing that is given out at every service generates an energy that touches every person present and goes out beyond the walls of the building, carrying the blessing of the spirit beings who have gathered around.

## FINDING AND VISITING A SPIRITUALIST CHURCH

The simplest way to find your nearest Spiritualist church is to look in your local phone book. If no church is listed you can contact a national Spiritualist organisation (see Useful Addresses section) who will be able to tell you of any churches in your area.

Anyone can go into a Spiritualist church. You don't have to be a member and no charge is made. Newcomers are always welcome. Most churches have Sunday services, but times do vary so check. There will also probably be other activities during the week. Spiritual healing is freely available.

Don't be nervous about entering a church. You won't see anything spooky and the furniture won't go flying around. Services are conducted under normal light and no one ever says, 'Is there anybody there?'

Don't be put off if the first medium you see is disappointing. Try another week, or visit another church. If you are looking for evidence or hoping for contact with a particular person you will sooner or later find what you are seeking, but be patient – it may take time.

Talk to people and don't be afraid to ask questions if there is anything you don't understand. Keep an open mind about everything you hear, consider it carefully but make up your own mind. And remember that messages can be inaccurate and even the spirits don't know everything.

Obviously, Spiritualism is not right for everybody and you may decide that your pathway lies elsewhere. But, hopefully, you will discover something to help you on your spiritual journey and give you comfort and food for thought.

# CHAPTER 4

# *Love is the Link*

As time went on I began giving private sittings (or consultations) as well as taking church services. This kept me very busy and I found it increasingly difficult to juggle the demands of my psychic work with my job as a secretary in a publishing company. I was forced to make a decision. It had to be one or the other. So I decided to give up my job and become a full-time medium.

A few years after this, fulfilling a long-held ambition, my husband and I decided to leave London behind and move to a more rural location. After much searching we found a house in Surrey, near the Hampshire border. The move meant losing touch with some old friends and some of the churches I served but it brought me new contacts and I soon found myself even busier than I had been before. I expanded the scope of my work to include the teaching of mediumship and psychic development, but the private sittings continued to be – and still are – my first love.

All sorts of people come to see me, men and women, young and old, people from all walks of life. They come for a variety of purposes. Some of them have been bereaved and are hoping to hear from the person who has died, but it would be a mistake to imagine that everyone who goes to see a medium has this same motive. In fact, I would estimate that only about half my sitters fall into this category. Some come out of curiosity, just to see what happens and who comes through. Provided they are sincere enquirers, I never mind this. I was full of curiosity myself once. Seeking, probing, asking questions is part of our spiritual search. Then there are those who come because they have a problem in their lives and are seeking advice from the spirit world on how to handle it. Many of them want me to foretell their future. 'Am I going to get married?' 'How many children am I going to have?' Foretelling the future is really not what Spiritualism is about, although the spirits do provide advice when it is necessary. The whole question of how much we should rely on them to guide us or to predict the future is one I will return to in a later chapter. But for now I want to talk about my most basic role as a medium, acting as an intermediary for those in the spirit world who wish to communicate with those they love on earth.

## MESSAGES OF LOVE

The death of a loved one is often a devastating blow. In this materialistic age many people assume that death is the end, that they will never see that person again and that, however deeply they are grieving, all they can do is to pick up the pieces of their lives and carry on as best they can.

But for others, their grief makes them start to question. What if there is something beyond? What is he – or she – is with me now, watching and listening? Some deep instinct, which is their own spirit within them, tells them that this is so. In many cases, they sense the person's presence. Maybe they catch a glimpse of something out of the corner of their eye but, when they turn to look, there is no one there. Strange, they think. I wonder … No, it's just my imagination. Then their thoughts turn to some of the stories they have heard about those weird people called mediums, who claim to be able to speak to the dead, and they think, *There's probably nothing in it but I may as well give it a try.* And that's when I get a nervous phone call saying, 'What do you do exactly?' or 'Can you make my granny appear?' I have to explain that, unfortunately, I can't make anyone appear. I do not sit in the dark, I do not hold hands with them round a table, I do not even go into trance. All I do is talk to the sitters, passing on the information being transmitted to me.

Before I can give a sitting, or a reading as it is sometimes called,

I have to prepare myself. I do this by spending a few minutes in the room where I work, opening my psychic senses and attuning my mind to my guides. I know that they will have been very busy behind the scenes, bringing together the spirits who are going to communicate with the sitter and giving them instructions on how to do it – the spirits have to learn this, just as we do. The guides also prepare the room where the sitting is to take place. They build up the energy, thus creating a force field around the medium in which the vibrations are heightened so that the communication can take place. As I sit waiting I am always very much aware of this heightened energy that comes into the room. Often the communicators will start arriving some time before the sitter and I feel the room filling up with people. In fact, if I don't feel anyone coming I get worried because this usually means the sitter is delayed or isn't going to turn up!

Some sitters are nervous when they arrive and I have to reassure them that nothing spooky is going to happen. If it is their first sitting I take a little time to explain to them a bit about how mediumship works, so that they will know what to expect.

In a typical sitting, the spirits who communicate will be people the sitter has known and loved: parents, grandparents, partners, children or friends. Other spirits may come as well, perhaps more distant relatives they never met, or who died before they were born. They are all drawn by the link of love and are there to say 'I am here and I care about you.' Guides will also present themselves to give their blessings and advice on the spiritual aspect of life.

Many sitters are already aware of the spirit people and just need me to act like a telephone operator, relaying the messages. Others are seeking evidence to convince them that the contact is genuine. The spirits understand this and co-operate in providing this evidence. They will endeavour to give me a picture of what they look like and a general sense of their personality. They then try to provide me with as much information about themselves as they can, including little personal details, anything the sitter knew about them and will recognise. Though these things might sound trivial to anyone else, to the recipient they speak volumes. A few examples will indicate what I mean.

I described Margaret's grandmother to her, saying that she was speaking of a fur stole. Apparently that very morning, Margaret had framed a picture of her grandmother wearing that stole. On another occasion a child who came back to her grandmother described the dress in which she had been buried, and I heard the words 'little stars around her picture'. The grandmother explained to me that she had a framed picture of her grand-daughter whom she called her 'little star'. At Christmas time she had put decorations, in the form of little stars, around the picture. And a seventeen-year-old boy who had died of meningitis spoke of his fondness for sport, adding that he had wanted to go skiing but had never had the opportunity. 'I haven't found any snow here yet,' he told his mother, who, despite her sadness, had to laugh for the remark reminded her of his sense of humour.

A communicator may give a characteristic expression. After Jim's mother died his father, who had died many years before his mother, came through to say that they were together again. 'She's with her mother,' he said, 'and the two of them haven't stopped nattering.' 'Nattering' is not a word I ever use, but it was apparently a favourite word of Jim's father's.

A friend's mother gave a brief message about some papers that she said would be found 'in the bottom of a drawer'. Shortly before this lady died, she had been anxious about some important financial documents which she believed had been stolen. When my friend was clearing out her flat, he found them at the bottom of the drawer, as his mother had said.

Sarah's father told her that he had been there when she had been sorting out her wardrobe and he had seen lots of clothes hanging around the walls of a room. He mentioned a bright-pink suit and the name Karrie. The previous week, Sarah had indeed sorted out her wardrobe and had hung up a selection of clothes for her sister to borrow. Her sister had selected a bright-pink suit – and her name was Karrie. He went on to talk about a silver cigarette lighter and a pair of silver cufflinks, items which Sarah told me he had left to her two sons. Her father also spoke of her mother, who he said was at that moment doing something in the garden. On checking, Sarah discovered that at the time of the sitting her mother had been in the greenhouse watering the plants.

The evidence given by the spirits may concern something that is going on in the life of the sitter. Even something as simple as 'you've just bought a new pair of shoes' or 'you had a row with your husband yesterday' indicates that the spirits are around and are fully aware of what is going on in our lives. One young couple were surprised when I gave them the message, from the wife's brother, 'He likes the new tiles you've put up in the kitchen.' Marion's father gave me a picture of a birthday cake, telling her that he would be there at his grandson's birthday party the following day.

Some couples use codes as a means of proving survival, arranging that whichever one of them dies first will try to come back and communicate the code to the other. The American medium, John Edward, asked me to give him a sitting over the phone and, although I don't normally do this, I agreed to try. I was aware of his mother and received the words 'your mother is your guiding light'. John later told me that he and his mother had arranged three codes between them, and the phrase 'guiding light' was an integral part of one of them. He has now received the other two codes, but he had to wait several years for them, which proves how difficult it can be for the spirits to transmit a particular message, even to a medium!

## EMOTIONAL REUNIONS

For a person who has never had a sitting before, to be given evidence that those they love still exist and are happy and at peace brings great comfort. I am quite used to people bursting into tears, but I don't mind because I know they are tears of emotion and joy.

Margaret came to see me following the death of her mother.

'Having sittings has helped me tremendously,' she told me. 'The first time I came to you I was a bit apprehensive, wondering what was going to happen and whether I was doing the right thing. I sort of knew she was there but I just needed it confirmed and needed to know she was all right. Once I had that, I felt that a great burden had been lifted. It helped me in the grieving process. I had been seeing a hypnotherapist, which had made a feel a bit better but I wasn't satisfied. I felt there was something missing. After the sitting, I felt complete.'

Many sitters are holding in their minds the memory of their loved ones as they were at the end of their lives: old, frail or in pain. They are relieved to learn that once the spirit is free of the body this pain leaves them and they become whole again. 'It's wonderful,' the spirits often tell me. 'I feel so well and strong.'

When Kareen came to see me I tuned in to her son Ben, who was twelve when he passed into the spirit world. Ben was accompanied by Kareen's mother, who told me, 'He's climbing about all over the place!' When the sitting was over, Kareen told me that Ben, who had muscular dystrophy, had spent most of his short life in a wheelchair. 'He was incredibly accepting and tolerant of what he had to put up with,' she said. 'But, of course, he would have loved to have been able to run and climb and do all the things boys do.' 'Now he can,' I told her. And it seemed from what Kareen's mother said that he was making up for lost time!

Sittings are of great comfort in cases where a person has died suddenly and there has been no opportunity to say goodbye. The sitter may be burdened with guilt.

'I should have gone to the hospital that day,' Maureen told me, in tears. 'I knew my father was very ill but he wasn't expected to die so soon. I had things to do so I told him I'd go the next day, but it was too late. He died in the night. I've regretted it ever since. Please tell him I'm sorry.' 'You don't need me to tell him,' I informed her. 'He can hear you. And he understands. You did everything you could for him and you don't need to feel guilty because you weren't there at the very end.' Knowing this, Maureen was able to release herself from the guilt she had been carrying for so long and to get on with her life.

If all this sounds very sombre, I should perhaps add that the spirits have a great sense of humour. One woman asked whether her father had met her mother in the spirit world. Back came the reply, 'Yes, and she's still not speaking to me!' Apparently they had parted acrimoniously and had still not made it up, which shows that it's not all love and harmony in the spirit world!

Although relatives often worry about how to arrange the funeral of their loved ones in accordance with their wishes or how to dispose of their ashes, the spirits show little concern about such things. One woman apologised to her father that she hadn't attended his funeral, which she felt had not been the sort of service he would have chosen. Her father quipped, 'Tell her I didn't bother to go either!' She had held a small private ceremony for him in her home, where she sang his favourite songs. He had been present at this and it had given him much pleasure.

Nigel had been deliberating for a long time about where he should scatter his mother's ashes. His mother came through, with a mixture of affection and amusement, to advise him as to which of the places he was considering she preferred. But she added, 'I really don't mind. Just tell him to get those ashes disposed of – I'm tired of looking at them!'

I occasionally have sittings myself, partly because I enjoy being on the receiving end for a change, partly because it gives my spirit friends a chance to get things across to me that perhaps they are not able to say to me direct. Though some of these sittings have been disappointing, many have been of tremendous value and given me encouragement and comfort at times when I was most in need. My grandmother and my parents have been the most frequent communicators, their messages being typical of their personalities.

But sometimes I have been surprised by some unlikely person making himself known like an unexpected guest turning up at a party. One incident in particular sticks in my mind. I once had a sitting with a medium called Bill Marie in which he said to me, 'I have a man here called Steele and he's saying "Red Riding Hood".' Though Bill had no idea what this could mean, it made perfect sense to me. When I was about four, my parents had a business associate called Steele. I only met Mr Steele once in my life, and on that occasion I was wearing a red coat with a hood. On seeing me, he laughed and said I looked like Red Riding Hood. I knew nothing about this man and there was nothing else he could have communicated to Bill that would have meant anything to me, but these words immediately recalled that memory.

## WHEN SITTINGS FAIL

Mediums are not machines and, although they can to some extent turn their ability on and off at will, there are times when it doesn't work at all. If I am unwell or very tired I am unable to tune in because I cannot raise my energy to the level needed to link in to the spirits. Whenever I feel I am not in a fit state to work, I cancel the sitting rather than attempt to do it and do it badly.

Unfortunately, there are mediums who 'make it up' when they are having a bad day, waffling on about anything that comes into their heads rather than admit that there is no spirit contact there. I consider this not only dishonest, but an insult to the sitter and to the spirit world. In any sitting there are bound to be some things the medium says that the sitter cannot understand or spirits who cannot be identified. But, allowing for this, the information given should in the main make sense and ring true to the sitter. If it doesn't the sitting clearly isn't working, in which case the only solution is to say so and abandon the attempt.

There are many reasons why communication may not be successful, and these are not all the fault of the medium. Atmospherics play a part: stormy, overcast conditions are not good. And some spirits are better communicators than others. The sitter's frame of mind also plays an important part. I don't want anyone to accept everything I say without question, but an overly critical attitude –

which I cannot help but sense, even if it is not expressed in words – has an inhibiting effect on the spirits and on me.

Sitters are sometimes disappointed when a special person they were hoping to hear from doesn't come through to them, but mediums cannot call spirits up if they are unable or unwilling to come. Some spirits fail to communicate because of the difficulties involved. They may not be available at that particular time – they don't spend their entire existence hovering around us! Alternatively, they may be present but unable to come through that particular medium. Even on earth, it can be hard to communicate with certain people if we are not on their wavelength. This is especially true when the means of communication is a mental one. Should you have this experience, don't assume that the person concerned has passed beyond reach. Try again with another medium and you may have more luck.

There are a few unfortunate people who never seem to be able to get a successful sitting. They go round from one medium to another and every session is blank. I feel sorry for these people, who are often doing their best to be co-operative. 'Is it my fault?' they ask. 'What am I doing wrong?' I have to explain, as tactfully as I can, that although they are not deliberately putting obstacles in the way, they are adversely affecting the conditions. I have spoken of the force field that the guides create around me, within which the vibrations are heightened. This force field is built up of energy supplied by the spirits, the medium and the sitter. When sitters are deeply depressed, as they may be if they have suffered a recent bereavement, this lowers the vibrations. Nervousness also has a disruptive effect. Those who are very materialistic in their thoughts and attitudes will set up a mental barrier which feels to me like a brick wall. This is not to say that communication is impossible under these circumstances but it means I have to work a lot harder to get anything through.

## ANIMALS IN THE SPIRIT WORLD

It seems to me absurd that some churchmen deny that animals have souls. This attitude has contributed to the cruelty shown to our lesser brethren down the centuries since it implies that they have no feelings and that therefore we have the right to exploit them. Of course animals have souls. They survive death and, when they are deeply attached to their owners, they are looked after in the spirit world and stay there until their owners go to join them.

I adore cats, and one of the great loves of my life was Delilah, a sweet, gentle grey cat with amber eyes. I called her 'the cat who came to dinner' because she originally came to me for a month while her owners were abroad and somehow never got around to going back to them.

Delilah and I had many happy years together, during the course of which we never had a cross word. Only in one respect was she a disappointment. Cats are supposed to be psychic, but Delilah showed no indication of any psychic ability whatsoever. She dozed contentedly through my sittings. No spirit being even penetrated her consciousness. She was far more interested in her next meal.

When she was only twelve years old her health began to fail. She developed heart problems and kidney failure and became pitifully thin and weak. Eventually I had to do what, in the circumstances, was the kindest thing I could do for her. The day she was put to sleep was one of the saddest days of my life. I cried for weeks afterwards, missing her weight on my lap, the way her tail shot up when she saw me coming, and the appreciative purr when I tickled her under the chin.

I sent up a prayer 'upstairs'. 'Take care of her for me. Let her be happy.' Several times I saw her in my home. Gradually her presence faded, but I was told that my mother was looking after her for me. This surprised me because my mother was not a 'cat' person. When I queried this, I was told, 'She's doing her best' and I knew that Delilah, with her irresistible charm, had won her over. Occasionally, when my mother comes to see me now, she has Delilah with her, looking fit and healthy. One day I hope to see my beloved pet again because of the very special bond we had.

Cats and dogs often feature in my sittings and are brought back to their owners by those who are looking after them. I have even seen the spirit form of a pet rabbit! Like humans, animals leave behind their illnesses and weaknesses and have a happy existence in a place where they are lovingly cared for.

## SPIRITUAL AWAKENING THROUGH GRIEF

Great though the pain is of losing someone we love, sometimes it leads to a spiritual awakening. Grief can be the key that unlocks the door to our inner self. I have seen so many people transformed in this way. Their bereavement has led them first to me or to another medium in order to make that precious contact and to be reassured that there is a life beyond. But from this they have gone on to find the spirit within themselves. And this has enabled them to achieve things they would not have thought possible – to develop their own mediumship and other spiritual gifts, to teach and to heal others.

Margaret, whose words I quoted earlier, went on to become a healer. Kareen undertook an adventurous trek across the Himalayas in order to raise money for Whizzkids, a charity which makes specially designed wheelchairs for disabled children and had supplied one for her son Ben.

Tana had a beautiful experience which was the incentive to start her spiritual work.

I woke up one night and saw my father by my bed. He was just standing there looking very intently at me. I wasn't frightened. He had four or five halos of light around him. Later, I was told that these were astral colours. Then he gradually faded away. Seeing him like that was a great comfort. I know he's still very close to me. I had always been interested in spiritual things but after that I started reading books on every aspect of psychic phenomena. Now I'm hoping to become a healer. I feel I have to give something back. I believe he came to me as he did in order to set me on my pathway.

Julie suffered a tragic loss when her daughter Janine, aged twenty-seven, was killed in a road accident. She was cycling to college when a lorry turned a corner. The driver failed to see her because she was in his 'blind spot' and she was knocked off her bike and killed instantly. Janine was an exceptional young woman, and Julie wrote to me about her.

She was beautiful, inside and out. She spoke five languages and had completed her university studies in the Chinese language and was one of the top students in her course of traditional Chinese medicine and acupuncture. She had been a very centred person since childhood, emotionally balanced and exuding a gentle calm. Her friends often said that she radiated light. To me she was my best friend, as well as being like a second mum to my son Dominic, who is eleven years younger. To her family, the devastation is beyond words. To me, her mother, the pain of losing her physically would have been unbearable had I not had knowledge (not belief but *knowledge*) that existence continues after the death of the body.

After Janine died, I was one of the first mediums Julie saw. She later wrote to me again.

You described her exactly and mentioned her boyfriend and that I should look for a pair of 'mobile' earrings. When I went through her things I found a pair of earrings that looked like a mobile (a sculpture, not a phone!). I discovered that her boyfriend had given her these. You also mentioned some purple flowers by her picture. These were dried flowers from her funeral. In another sitting some months later, Janine referred to an article in a magazine. I did not understand the significance of this but the following day I was approached by a magazine who wanted to write an article about her.

Julie also told me about evidence she received from other mediums.

> Peter Close, in a demonstration of clairvoyance at the Spiritualist Association of Great Britain, described Janine and said she was saying that her death had been painless and instantaneous and that I should not worry about this, as in fact I had been doing. Coral Polge, the psychic artist, drew an unmistakably recognisable picture of my mother. Shirley Smith, the medium who was working with Coral on that occasion, gave her name as Agnes, saying, 'She is bringing with her a young lady who went over with head injuries.' This young lady was telling her that a very special day was coming soon. It was my birthday a few days later and Janine had always made a fuss of my birthday.
>
> Since then I have had several wonderful, evidential sittings with various mediums and as my own sensitivity has developed I have been able to make direct contact with Janine. It is wonderful! It is like a telephone line – we can 'dial' each other direct, we don't seem to need 'telephone exchanges' (mediums) any more! Sometimes when I feel her very close I still have to cry – the tears just have to flow. Although it is very emotional, it is a feeling of pure joy.

Julie organises concerts and other events in commemoration of her daughter to raise money for charity. She became involved in an organisation called RoadPeace in her campaign to have extra mirrors fitted on lorries to cover the 'blind spot' so that such accidents can be prevented, and she appeared on behalf of this organisation on the BBC programme *Watchdog*. She is working on a book about Janine's life and has also trained to be a medium, work which she finds deeply satisfying and rewarding. All these things she has been able to accomplish because Janine is working with her.

Julie's story demonstrates what is to me the most important aspect of the contact mediums are able to provide with the spirit world. Of course it is, as Julie says, wonderful to know that those we love are with us and that there is in reality no such thing as death, only transformation to a higher life. But once we have this knowledge, rather than endlessly seeking more 'messages' and further proof and reassurance, we have to use this knowledge to enrich our lives, to further our spiritual progress. If we do this, those we love will be walking beside us, bringing their love and their strength, so that we can go forward together.

## FINDING AND CONSULTING A MEDIUM

As I have already indicated, mediums vary tremendously in their ability. I personally have never come across any fraudulent mediums, although of course they do exist. You should be extremely wary of anyone who pretends to have a one hundred per cent success rate or makes any extravagant claims. The vast majority of mediums are sincere but, unfortunately, many of them are not very good. In order to avoid disappointment you should be very selective about who you see.

There are a number of things you can do to help ensure the success of the sitting. Before you go, if possible attend a few meetings at a Spiritualist church and read about the subject in order to familiarise yourself with the basic mechanism by which communication works. This will help you to understand what is going on and to appreciate the difficulties involved so that you do not have unreasonable expectations.

Approach the sitting in a calm frame of mind. There is nothing to be nervous about! Keep an open mind, not treating every word as gospel truth (mediums can be wrong or inaccurate) but not being overly critical either. If there is anything you don't under-stand, don't be afraid to ask questions. Should you be told of any communicators whom you don't recognise or be given information that you don't know about, talk to other members of the family. They may be able to shed more light on the situation.

If you are hoping to hear from a particular person, send out a loving thought to them. But if the medium doesn't mention this person, don't be too disappointed. Remember that there are various reasons why it may be impossible for them to get through. They may make contact later, through the same medium or through someone else. Accept those who do come, even if they are people you were not expecting. Every spirit that comes has come in love and wants to be accepted.

Should you be one of those unfortunate people who just cannot seem to get a successful sitting from any medium, don't give up in despair. There is something you can do. Examine your attitude. Are you being too demanding? I am not saying that you should be gullible – far from it – but a sitting should be viewed as an experiment in which the sitter and the medium work together, rather than as a trial in which the medium has to prove her ability.

If you find it difficult to believe in a spirit world, at least try to open your mind to the possibility that there might be something in it. Read about the subject and consider the evidence that has been accumulated over the years. Most of all, try to raise your level of consciousness so that you do not disrupt the force field I spoke off. You may not think of yourself as a religious or a spiritual person, but we all have a spirit within. Hard though you may find it, try to pray or to meditate so that your spirit can awaken. And as this happens, so those who love you in the spirit world will be able to communicate with you.

Whatever your initial attitude you may need to see more than one medium before you succeed in finding one who can give you a wholly satisfying sitting. This is partly because of the variable standard of mediumship and partly because no medium can be equally successful with every sitter. But each sitting should give you something of value and should, at the very least, stimulate your curiosity to investigate further.

Take notes of all the sittings you have – you never remember it all. You may wish to tape record the session, but ask the medium's permission to do this as some mediums find the tape recorder inhibiting. However, bear in mind the curious fact that psychic energy affects electrical equipment. When sitters bring tape recorders it frequently happens that the machine refuses to work, or else they get home to find that the tape is blank. This has occurred so often that I now tell people that they are quite welcome to make a recording, but I refuse to take responsibility if it doesn't come out!

Finally, remember that spirit communication works on the link of love. The more love you send out, to the medium and the spirits, the more they will be able to help you in return.

# CHAPTER 5

# From the Spirit Side

What is it like for those who have left the earth behind and passed into the next world? What do they feel when they come back to visit us? Sitters often ask me such questions and I share their curiosity. I do not have all the answers. I doubt whether we can ever understand what their existence is really like until we get to that place ourselves. But from the information that has been given, through mediums, over the past hundred years and from what I myself have been told by the spirits, I can but offer my impressions of how things appear from their point of view.

## THE SPIRITS' NEED TO COMMUNICATE

Perhaps the most reassuring fact, and something that the spirits tell us over and over again, is that the process of death is nothing to fear. Dying is as simple and painless as falling asleep. Everyone is met at the point of death, usually by a parent or by someone they have loved. These reunions bring great joy. I am often told, 'My husband came to meet me' or 'I'm with my parents.' An elderly man whose last years had been spent in loneliness told me, 'I've now got all my family round me'.

People who had no belief in an afterlife while on earth are often very surprised at finding themselves still alive, and are eager to tell their families that they are still around. One man who had disapproved of Spiritualism returned to his daughter at a Spiritualist church service admitting, 'I wouldn't have been seen dead in a place like this!'

Those who die suddenly – as a result, perhaps, of a stroke or heart attack – may be shocked at finding themselves on the other side. For those who die violently, such an abrupt transition is traumatic. It may be a while before they realise that they have left the earthly life. There are accounts of accident victims standing at the scene of the accident wondering why no one can see them. They are puzzled when they look down on the physical body and shocked when it dawns upon them that it is their own body they are seeing. But since nothing happens that is not foreseen by the spirit world, there is always someone on hand to meet these people and to help them to come to terms with their new state.

But though the transition is so easy, it is sometimes hard for the spirits to release their attachment to the earth. A materialistic person who set great store by their money or possessions might be held back by their concern over these things. Ghost stories that tell of misers haunting the place where their money was kept hold more than a hint of truth. But generally it is not so much possessions that make it difficult for the spirits to release themselves as the people they leave behind.

Gillian told me about the death of her father.

My sister phoned to tell me that our father had suffered a massive heart attack. I went straight home and started to pray. My hands locked together and I couldn't move them. I looked towards the window and saw outside a brilliant white light which moved up and out of sight. My hands then released and I knew he had gone. Later, my sister phoned to tell me that he had died at exactly that time.

Later, Gillian received a message from her father through a medium, telling her that he couldn't go away and rest until he'd thanked her for helping him to pass. Her father's mind had been in turmoil, part of him wanted to go but he didn't want to leave his family. Gillian has since received many messages from her father and knows that he is now settled and happy.

After my mother died, I felt her around all the time. I knew that she was anxious and was trying to warn me of something, but I could never quite catch what she was saying. Then one day, just as I was waking up, I heard her say, 'Take care of Harry.'

Harry was her brother, with whom she had lived. I promised her that I would do so. He was in his eighties and her death had hit him very hard. But my promise didn't seem to put my mother's mind at rest. I still felt her very close and knew that for some reason her anxiety was preventing her from settling down in the spirit world and being with my father. A while later I understood her concern, when my uncle was taken seriously ill and had to go into hospital. I looked after him until he was better and helped him to sell the house he and my mother had shared and move to somewhere smaller and more convenient. This made my mother happy. I was conscious of her relief and knew that she felt able to let go. Now when I feel her with me, I sense a peace and happiness and know she is giving me her blessing.

Mediums are often accused of calling up the dead, but it is more a case of them calling us up. Their need to communicate with us is as great as our wish to contact them. When people find themselves in the spirit world their immediate need, after they have recovered from their surprise, is to get back to those they have left behind, to tell them not to grieve. And because in that world spirits travel by the power of thought, it is this that draws them back to their homes and families. This is why, after people die, their loved ones on earth often feel them close.

The spirits can see their relatives and they know that they are missed – or not, as the case may be. They can see into people's minds and discover exactly what everyone really thought of them! When someone is crying or upset the spirits naturally want to comfort them, but in most cases they cannot make themselves seen or heard. This is saddening and frustrating for them.

The spirits try to draw attention to their presence in any way they can, sometimes by making noises in the house or moving small objects. Sitters often tell me of incidents such as door handles rattling, footsteps being heard or objects turning up in unlikely places where they couldn't possibly have got by themselves. People are sometimes frightened when things like this happen, but it is not the spirits' intention to cause fear – they are simply trying to let someone know they are there.

Spirits cannot physically move anything in our world, so they have to move things by the power of thought. Anyone who has seen the film *Ghost* will have the idea. Joan Wadham gave me an amusing example of this.

When my mother was alive she was always finding coins on the ground when she was out walking, mostly £1 coins. After her death we kept finding 1p pieces in the oddest places. When I went to the solicitors to sign over her flat to my sister, as soon as I stepped out of the car I saw a 1p piece on the ground. And I would find a 1p piece on the carpet where I had just vacuumed. This sort of thing also happens to my sister and to a friend my mother was very fond of. In fact, every time something important happens or there is an anniversary, or if I am feeling upset or very down, a 1p piece appears. When the twins were born I asked my friend whether she thought my mother knew there were twins. Ten minutes later, there was a 2p piece on the counter I had just cleaned down!

Another method the spirits use is to create a familiar smell. This is a very common phenomenon. I am frequently told by sitters that they have smelt their father's pipe tobacco or their mother's favourite brand of perfume. How the spirits manage to do this is an intriguing mystery they have never divulged to me!

Because psychic energy can affect electrical equipment, where there is a spirit presence appliances such as televisions and computers may malfunction or suffer from interference. There have been reports of people holding telephone conversations with spirits. I have never come across any instances of this but I was told an interesting story by Astrid.

My mother passed on very suddenly. I woke up in the middle of the night after her death because I heard the telephone ringing, just once. Two nights later, my husband had a similar experience and two nights after that my sister also heard the phone ring once. I took this as a sign from my mother because, very peculiar to her, whenever she went away she would call one of her children, letting the phone ring just once. We would know that it was her and could ring her back so as not to incur costs for the person our mother was staying with.

What better indication could Astrid's mother have given to let her daughter know that she had arrived safely?

If the spirits cannot reach the person they want to speak to directly they may make themselves known to someone else who can pass on a message for them. Kareen told me how she saw her grandfather after his death.

I was lying in bed, crying and thinking of him when I felt someone stroking my hair. At first I was a bit frightened then I heard his voice in my head, 'It's all right. It's grandad. Tell your mother I'm all right.' He had died suddenly and my mother was distraught, but I thought, *If I tell her she'll think I've gone bananas!* But I felt I had to pass on the message, so I just said to her quietly, 'Grandad came to see me last night and he wants you to know he's all right.' I was amazed at how she accepted this and how much it calmed her.

Another way in which the spirits make contact is through dreams. When we sleep, the spirit self leaves the physical body. In this state we can meet with spirits face to face and talk to them because we have temporarily entered their sphere of consciousness. Usually we forget about such happenings when we wake up. But some of the vivid dreams we have are memories of these astral meetings.

Claudia had a dream of her father, in which he said that he needed to speak to her and asked her to find a medium. When she told him she didn't know one, he said, 'Ask your friend Anna.'

Claudia did so, and Anna brought her to me.

It is those who die suddenly who have the most urgent desire to get in touch with those they have left behind. Having been so abruptly snatched away from their families, they have so much they want to say, unfinished business to sort out, love to express.

'I'm sorry I left things in such a mess,' was the message of one road accident victim to his wife. She admitted that she was having problems in sorting out his financial affairs, but her greatest concern was that she never had the chance to say goodbye to him. 'You never have to say goodbye,' I told her. 'He's telling me that he's going to be around for as long as you need him. He'll never be very far away.'

In the same way that sitters sometimes wish to ask forgiveness from a spirit loved one, the spirits may wish to ask forgiveness from those on earth. In some cases they need to do this before they can be at peace. One woman's grandfather came back, full of remorse, because he had abused her as a child. 'He's suffering because of what he did to you,' I told her. 'Good!' she responded. I can't say I blame her for this reaction, but I hope that one day she might find it in her heart to let go of the bitterness, for both their sakes.

Some of the most moving examples of this need to seek forgiveness have come from those who have committed suicide. There is no judgement in the spirit world for those who take their own lives. They are met with sympathy and understanding. But they are often stricken with remorse and feel a desperate need to communicate this to their families and to explain what drove them to take such drastic action.

One teenage boy came through at a sitting to a woman who was a friend of his mother's, asking her to pass on a message to his mother. He wanted her to know how sorry he was for the pain he had caused her. On reflection, he said, he appreciated that he should have stayed and worked out his problems, but at the time he had been too depressed to see any way out. He reassured his mother that he was well and was receiving healing, and asked her to go and see a medium so that he could speak further to her. 'He was the last person I expected to hear from,' the sitter commented, but she promised to pass on the message to the boy's mother.

Very often, any regret the spirits feel is for the lack of love they showed in their lives. Again and again I am asked to transmit messages along the lines of 'I did love you – I just didn't know how to show it.' Such sentiments come from strict parents, grandparents who were too reserved by nature to demonstrate their affection, or from people who let small, unimportant disagreements spoil their relationships or who were too absorbed in their own lives to notice the needs of those around them. It is, perhaps, a warning to us all that we should show our love while we are on earth so that we won't feel regrets when this life is over.

## LIFE IN THE SPIRIT WORLD

When people arrive in the spirit world they do not sprout wings. They exist in a spirit body which is a replica of their earthly body, but composed of a finer substance. I have already mentioned that the spirit body does not suffer from illness and weakness, and that for people who were ill when on earth there is great joy at being free from pain. Those who were disabled, like Kareen's little son Ben, are made whole. I was very moved when an elderly lady who had been blind in her last years wanted me to tell her daughter, 'At last I can see my grandchildren.' My uncle, who had driven everyone mad by refusing to wear his hearing aid, told me through another medium, 'I don't need this contraption any more!'

When the spirits return, initially they often give an impression of themselves as they were at the end of their lives. This is done for purposes of recognition. In the case of someone who dies at an advanced age, for instance, I might initially see her looking old and frail. Once I have described her and the sitter says, 'Yes, that's my grandmother', or whoever, that picture then fades and I get an impression of the spirit as she is now – restored to full vigour and looking as she did in the prime of her life.

As regards the feelings and personalities of spirits, they are the same as they were on earth, which is why I talk of spirit people rather than entities or ghosts. The spirits' love for their families and friends endures, and I am very conscious of this love when the spirits come to me. I can only convey the words, but I wish I could pass on to sitters the depth of emotion they communicate. There will often be characteristic traits that help sitters to identify a loved one. Your old granny who liked to fuss around you will still be fussing and telling you to wrap up warmly in winter. Your friend who thought she always knew better than you how to run your life will still be giving her advice – though you don't necessarily have to take it.

This is not to say that people do not change once they reach the spirit world. They can, because they are in a spiritual environment where even the most materialistically minded individuals cannot but respond to the love and light around them. As time goes on they become wiser (though not all-knowing), more loving and more tolerant. But it is a gradual development, and the rate at which people develop depends upon their willingness to learn and progress.

The particular dimension of the astral world which most of our loved ones inhabit is called in Spiritualism the Summerland. It is described by the spirits as being surprisingly like our own world. It has countryside and parks, houses and cities, but everything is more rarefied and more beautiful. There is a soft light that permeates everything and does not hurt the eyes, but there are no mechanical things like cars, telephones and computers and there is no need to work for a living.

Summerland is, in a sense, a material world in that it appears real and solid to those living there, but it is composed of finer material than the earth and vibrates at a higher frequency. But there is an even more important difference, and this is a difficult concept to grasp. The astral world is a world of thought. Every-thing that exists there – the scenery, the houses, the clothes that are worn (spirit people tend to wear clothes similar to the ones they wore on earth) – is brought into being by the wishes and desires of the inhabitants.

But this idyllic existence is not all rest and enjoyment. There is work to do in the astral world, though, of course, it is work of a spiritual nature. It may take the form of bringing light to those on earth, perhaps working with mediums or healers. It may involve going down into the lower regions to help those trapped there. It may be working on one's own spiritual development.

One aspect of the work, for those spirits who choose to do this, is keeping an eye on their earthly families. For as long as there is anyone on earth who cares about these spirits they will return, aiding us with their thoughts and their prayers and taking an interest in our lives. This does not mean that they are hovering around us every moment of the day. They get on with their own lives. But there is always a mental contact, like a telephone line that is always open.

Though the spirit people can see us, they do not expect us to see them. Nora told me about an encounter she had.

I woke up early one morning and found I was holding someone's hand. I thought at first it must be my son, then I realised that it couldn't be him at that time of day. Then I opened my eyes and looked up. It was my husband standing there. He was wearing a tweed jacket and open-necked shirt. His hair was black as it had been when he was young – he was seventy-two when he died. I was so shocked that I let go of his hand and went to throw my arms round him. 'What are you doing here?' I asked. Then I realised, from the look on his face, that he was more shocked than I was. I found myself laughing at his surprise.

## SITTINGS – FROM THE SPIRIT SIDE

I am often asked how the spirits know when someone is going to have a sitting, in order that they can turn up. They know because of the constant mental link they have with us. Even though, in their world, there is no time, this mental link enables them to be aware of our time. This is demonstrated by an amusing story given to me by Anna.

My mother lived in Bournemouth and her sister lived in Leeds. Her sister was taking an afternoon nap. She dreamed of their mother, who was talking to her. Her mother said, 'I'm sorry, but I have to leave you now. I have an appointment somewhere else.' With that she woke up and noticed that it was half past three. The next day she rang her sister (my mother) and told her about the dream. My mother told her that at three-thirty she was having a sitting with a medium and her mother came through!

The spirits are delighted when someone decides to have a sitting because this gives them the opportunity to communicate, an opportunity for which they may have been waiting eagerly for a long time. In fact, the idea may have come from them in the first place, having put the thought into the sitter's mind. But even then, getting through is not easy. To get an idea of what goes on behind the scenes, let us follow the story of an imaginary character – we'll call her Mary.

Mary dies in her eighties, after a long illness. She is met by her mother and taken to her new home in the spirit world, a house not unlike the one where her mother used to live. This is all very pleasant, but Mary knows that her daughter Jane will be grieving for her and she desperately wants to get back and tell her that all is well.

No sooner has she thought of Jane than she finds herself with her. Jane is crying and she longs to comfort her but she cannot do this. Jane cannot see her. She speaks to her but Jane cannot hear her voice. Mary touches her. Jane shivers and glances up. She has sensed her mother there but she is a little frightened and dismisses it, saying, 'It's just my imagination.'

But Mary persists, prompted by her own mother who knows something about these things. 'If you move something, she might take some notice,' Mary's mother says. And she shows Mary how to do this, by concentrating mental energy on the plant on the table. It requires a great effort but Mary is able to make the leaves flutter as if swayed by a breeze. Jane is startled. She checks to see whether there is a draught in the room, but there isn't. She begins to think that perhaps her mother is there after all.

With a great deal of mental persuasion Mary prompts Jane to visit a medium. Mary's mother and a host of other relatives decide to go along as well. Jane arrives at the medium's house feeling nervous but hopeful. Her mother and the rest of the family are there waiting for her. The guides are standing in the background, ready to assist. One of them leads Mary forward and tells her to try to link mentally with the medium by focusing her thoughts and trying to lock on to the medium's wavelength.

To Mary's relief, the medium is able to see her. She describes her to Jane, who is happy to acknowledge that it is her mother. Mary has a hundred things she wants to say to her. She wants to pour out her love to her daughter, to tell her not to grieve any more but to be happy for her. She wants to describe what the spirit world is like and talk about all the people she has met there. And she wants to send her love to Jane's family and to congratulate Jane's little son on passing his exams.

But there is so little time and she is so limited in what she can get across to the medium. To her disappointment, she discovers that some of the things she says the medium fails to pick up. Other things get distorted. Then there are so many other people, all wanting to get through. The guides are trying to sort them out so that they all have their turn, but some are impatient. Mary's sister, who was a bossy individual, elbows her way to the front of the queue. Sundry aunts and uncles have a go. Jane's grandfather, who was a shy, reserved chap, wants to say something but can't get a word in edgeways.

The sitting leaves Jane a little confused. She is convinced that her mother and the other members of the family were there but she wonders why her mother didn't refer to some of the major events going on in the family that she ought surely to have known about. She is surprised not to have heard from her grandfather, of whom she was very fond. But she feels happier and more at peace than she did before.

Mary is relieved at having made contact, though slightly disappointed not to have been able to say more. But she has stirred Jane's interest and hopes Jane will take it further, by either giving her mother the chance to communicate again, through another medium, or perhaps developing her own awareness so that they can speak to each other directly.

## ARE SPIRITS HELD BACK BY OUR GRIEVING?

Mediums sometimes say that by grieving for those who have died we hold them back and prevent them from finding peace in the spirit world. This is something that worries many sitters who have lost someone they loved dearly, so I feel I should say a few words about this. It is natural to grieve when someone you love dies. You need to express this emotion. In fact, suppressing it can cause much harm psychologically. It takes months or years to get over the death of a close friend or relative. In some cases, you never fully get over it. Though the knowledge that the person concerned is living in the spirit world is a consolation, it does not take away the sense of loss.

The person in spirit will understand your need to grieve and to shed tears. They themselves may be feeling some sadness at the separation and will therefore remain close by. How long they remain very close depends upon your needs and theirs. If there is a strong link of love they will never be far from your side. Problems arise when a person holds too tightly to someone who has passed into the spirit world, by constantly calling upon them and pleading with them not to go away. This makes it hard for the spirit to detach themselves from the earth and to settle into their new life because they will be worried about the one who is grieving.

Think of it this way. The soul is like a bird. If you keep it confined in a cage all the time it will pine. You have to open the cage door so that it can fly free into its natural environment. But if you have established a bond of love with that bird, it will return to you often and be your companion. In the same way, the best thing we can do for our loved ones who have died is to release them with our love, so that they can move into the astral plane, which is the soul's true home. Then, when they return to us, which they will do often, they will come back strong and happy, bringing with them the light of the spirit world.

The contact with those we love can continue for the rest of our lives. The spirits do not want us to be sorrowful for them. They want us to be happy and to live our lives to the full. Over time, as I have said, they learn and grow in that world and, if we also are learning and growing, we can progress together. I have sitters who come to see my regularly, about once a year. I am delighted to see how some of these people are finding fulfilment in their lives and I know their spirit loved ones are helping them in this.

Julie, who I mentioned earlier, is one of my regular sitters. She is now working as a medium herself and has a spiritual partnership with her daughter Janine, who works with her. Janine's death appeared a pointless tragedy and, of course, Julie will never cease to miss her daughter's physical presence. But I have sensed over the years how Janine herself has changed and developed since the first time she came through to me. The light she brings tells me how she has grown in wisdom and strength. Now she is reaching out, through Julie, to help others.

## WHEN SOMEONE YOU LOVE DIES

If someone you love has died, you may well sense them with you. Don't assume that this is your imagination. Acknowledge them by speaking to them, either aloud or in your mind. You may not hear any response but you may feel it in your mind and your heart. The spirit within you is in touch with the spirit of the one you love, so trust your intuition and that inner knowing that tells you they are near.

If you think you hear any strange noises or anything is moved, first look for a natural explanation. If you can't find one, it may well be that your spirit loved one is the cause. Don't be frightened by this. You wouldn't have been scared of that person when they were in the body so why should you be scared now? Again, acknowledge that you have noticed. Don't think they are going to suddenly appear before you or jump out at you from behind a door. You are much more likely to sense their presence than to see them. But if it should happen that you see them it will just be a fleeting glimpse – startling perhaps, but comforting rather than frightening.

If you sense that they want to communicate further with you, go and see a medium. Remembering the advice I have already given about making allowances for the difficulties of communication, if the first sitting is not successful, try again. You will be helping your spirit loved one as much as yourself.

## MAKING YOUR OWN CONTACT WITH LOVED ONES

You do not need to be a medium to make contact with those you love in the spirit world. Remember, you too are a spirit being so all you have to do is open your spiritual awareness.

Set aside a time when you can be quiet. Sit in the place you use to meditate. When you feel calm and centred, send out your thoughts to those you love in spirit. It may help to have photographs of them. Do not focus on any one particular person. Wait and see who you sense is there and accept that person. Talk to them in your mind. You may not hear them reply but you may feel a response inwardly. Or you may have just a feeling that they are there.

Obviously, it takes time to develop this ability and some people have more success than others. But most people, if they persevere, with love and trust can develop for themselves an inner knowing, a contact with those who are watching over them. And once you have established this companionship, nothing will ever take it away from you.

# CHAPTER 6

# Seeking Guidance

I have said that some people go to see a medium not because they want to contact someone who has died but because they are seeking advice or guidance in some aspect of their lives. The matters over which they seek this guidance are extremely varied. In some cases the help they ask for is on a spiritual level. They are not sure of their direction in life or how they can best use their talents and abilities. In other cases the issue is a material one, to do with money, home or career.

## SEEKING HELP WITH EMOTIONAL PROBLEMS

Some sitters come with deep and distressing problems. I never cease to be surprised at the burdens people carry and the fears and anxieties they endure, which are often masked behind a cheerful manner and a bright smile. Sometimes it is the ones who appear the most cheerful and outwardly calm who have the most difficult lives. I listen while they pour their hearts out to me and wish I had a magic wand I could wave to make all their troubles go away. But, unfortunately, I cannot do that.

In fact, as a medium it is not my job to provide solutions. I am not a counsellor, much less a miracle worker. Though, of course, I will offer a sympathetic ear, my task is not to speak on my own behalf but to pass on to sitters whatever their loved ones or guides in the spirit world wish me to say. I am acutely aware of my responsibility to be as clear a channel as possible and to attune to the highest spiritual level I can in order to receive accurate information. But I have to remind sitters that whatever advice does come through from the spirits, it is just that – advice. It is up to us to lead our own lives and make our own decisions. So to what extent should we depend upon the spirits to guide us? This is an important question and one that should be considered carefully by mediums and sitters alike.

A lot of the problems sitters bring to me concern relationships. 'Am I going to meet the man of my dreams?' they ask. 'Is my partner being unfaithful to me?' 'Should I divorce my wife?'

Pity the poor medium, confronted with these questions, the answers to which could change the course of the person's life irrevocably. What a responsibility! For, despite what I always say to people about making their own decisions, I know that many of them will accept my word, or the word of any medium they consult, without question and act upon it implicitly. And if the advice is wrong the consequences could be disastrous.

If I am not very careful how I handle these delicate situations I can find myself in a lot of trouble. Some years ago a man who came for a sitting admitted that he was having an affair with his wife's friend. He wanted to know if his wife suspected. The spirits refused to answer his question. They advised him instead to stop the affair and try to save his marriage. He went away disgruntled, since this was not what he wanted to hear.

The following week I received a request for a sitting from a woman who gave only her Christian name. During the course of the session it became apparent that she was the wife of the man I had seen previously. She told me that she thought he was having an affair and could I confirm this? This put me in a very difficult position. I have a rule, which I never break, of strict confidentiality. Where sittings are concerned I am, if you will excuse the expression, as quiet as the grave. I never repeat anything that passes between me and a sitter in private. Fortunately, the spirits were cleverer than me and managed to give her some advice without answering her question directly.

That was not the only occasion on which I have been caught in this particular minefield. Another time I gave a sitting to a woman whose father came through to me, giving some quite personal information about her relationship with her partner, with whom she was in the throes of an acrimonious separation. A few days later her partner rang me, demanding to know what her father had said about him! As always, I refused to divulge the information and he rang off. But I fully expected him to arrive on my doorstep and give me a punch on the nose!

Incidents like this make me very wary of trying to deal with people's emotional problems. But relationships are a major part of our lives and are often fraught with difficulties so it is only natural that, when sitters seek the advice of their spirit friends, this is one of the main issues that comes up. The spirits are well aware of our problems and heartaches and, because of the love they have for us, they will willingly give all the help they can, but there are certain spiritual laws they have to obey. They will not give information that would help the sitter to do anything immoral or anything that would hurt another person. Like me, they have to respect confidentiality. They will not give information that would be an unfair invasion of someone else's privacy. Also, they will not say anything that would fuel the fire in a dispute between partners. What they will do is give helpful insights into the situation, advising how it can be dealt with in the kindest way.

Whatever the communications that come through, you should remember if you are seeking guidance in this way that no medium can be one hundred per cent accurate. Sometimes mediums can be wildly inaccurate. The fact that certain things a medium says during the course of the sitting are correct does not mean that everything said can be relied upon. It should also be borne in mind that the spirits are not infallible. They may be a bit wiser than they were when they were on earth – but not in every case. Much depends on how they have progressed since going into the spirit world. They may also have access to information which you do not possess. But their opinions and personalities still colour the advice they give and, if you could hear spirit people talking, you might find that they don't agree with each other over the correct handling of a situation.

If, for instance, your strict old grandmother was implacably opposed to divorce when she was on earth, she may well advise you to stay with your marriage even if your husband is behaving badly. On the other hand, if you were to consult your recently deceased friend who had a much more modern outlook on life, she might advise you to throw him out! Your guides may take a different point of view altogether. Their approach is a spiritual one. Although they feel deeply for us, they are not caught up in human emotions and they consider what will be of greatest spiritual benefit for all the people concerned in a situation. It is up to you who you listen to, but in the end it's your life and you have to make up your own mind.

Claire came to me when she was going through a difficult divorce. She was frustrated that her husband was unwilling to reach an agreement over the sale of their home and the custody of their children. Her mother, from the spirit world, advised that she should pursue the matter through her solicitor and hold out for what was rightfully hers. But her guide explained that there was a karmic link between Claire and her husband which was at the root of the bitterness between them. Until the karma was resolved by forgiveness, he told her, they would not be able to settle the matter on the material level. Both these pieces of advice were true but Claire's mother was concerned with the down to earth aspect of the problem while the guide saw beyond this to the deeper spiritual issues involved.

The advice given by the guides has a ring of truth about it. Sitters instinctively know it to be right, even if they do not want to hear it. The guides' plea is always for us to try to act with love and compassion, however ill used or hard done by we feel. Sometimes sitters reject this because they are angry and resentful over a person or a situation and are not willing to see things from a spiritual perspective. That, of course, is their choice.

Quite often the advice given by the guides will be 'Go within yourself and the answer will come to you.' This may seem like an evasion on the part of the medium but it is actually just what the sitter needs to do. When we are confused or bogged down in emotional problems it is hard to be calm enough to connect with our own inner wisdom and the spirit within. But if we can still the outer mind, meditate and find that point of stillness, we discover that all the answers we need are there for us. This inner guidance is in the end what we must seek. Our spirit friends will support us, but we have to think for ourselves and take responsibility for our own actions.

Another point to bear in mind is that, if you have a fixed thought in your mind, the communication the medium receives can be distorted. I have spoken before about the importance of the sitter being in a calm, open-minded state, and this is never more important than when seeking help with emotional issues. If the sitter has a strong desire for the medium to give a particular answer to a question, the medium can inadvertently pick up this thought and think it comes from spirit.

One woman I knew many years ago was desperate to get back her husband, who had deserted her. She went round every medium she could find, asking them all if he was going to return. Nearly all of them reassured her that he was. She was bitterly disappointed when, after a long period of time, it became apparent that this was not going to happen, and she demanded to know why the spirits had let her down. In fact, it was more likely that her intense desire to receive a particular answer had clouded the mediums' minds and blocked any true communication. The issue eventually resolved itself. Last time I saw her she had met someone else and didn't want him back anyway!

## HEALTH ISSUES

An area of concern about which sitters frequently seek information is health. This is another potential minefield. Occasionally a sitter will ask a direct question like, 'Is my mother going to die?'

I try never to say anything that will cause sitters worry or alarm. I don't want them to go away feeling worse than when they arrived!

So I am very reluctant to give bad news of any kind and, as a rule, the spirits do not tell me when anyone is going to die. There are, however, rare occasions when they judge it right to give a warning that someone is going to pass into the spirit world, perhaps in the case of a person who is elderly or suffering a painful illness, for whom death would be a release. The sitters who are given this information are always those who are aware of the spirit world and know that they will be losing only the person's physical presence and that their spirit will live on. Even so, these messages are only ever given for a good reason, such as to allow the sitter to arrange the best possible care for the person or to spend time with them before they leave the earth. In these cases, I have to trust that, if the spirits give me this information, it is because the sitter wants the truth and is able to bear it. Obviously, though, communications like this have to be passed on with tact and kindness and with great care.

## PREDICTING THE FUTURE

I am often asked whether the spirits can predict the future. The answer is that they can see further along the road than we can, and the more highly evolved they are, the further they can see. However, they may not always be able or willing to tell us what is going to happen in any particular situation. There are times when the spiritual laws I have referred to forbid them to reveal what is to come. They are not allowed to interfere in our lives. Sometimes we need to undergo certain unpleasant experiences in order to learn and, if we were told what was going to happen and were able to avoid these experiences, then we wouldn't learn the lessons!

This raises the whole issue of whether everything in our lives is preordained or whether we create our own destiny – too big an issue to be discussed at length here. It is my belief, based on what I have been told by spirits, that the main events of our lives are mapped out in advance and that the most significant people in our lives are put in our path because we have a connection with them from past lives. But I do believe that we have some free will, mainly in the way in which we react to the things that happen to us and in whether or not we accept the opportunities with which we are presented.

The spirits do sometimes make predictions with uncanny accuracy – though these are not always welcomed. One of my sitters came to me wanting to know whether she was going to get a particular job she had set her heart on. I told her that she would be offered a temporary job instead, but that after a while she would be able to get back into the line of work she wanted to follow. She was very disappointed, but the next day she phoned me. She hadn't got the job but she had been offered a short-term assignment, covering for someone who was going on maternity leave. Though it wasn't exactly what she wanted she decided to accept it, trusting that she could afterwards resume her chosen career.

Sometimes the spirits take a very long-term view. I have had people come to me and say, 'Do you remember what you told me four years ago?' (I never do.) 'Well, it has come true!'

There is no time in the spirit world, so while I have known events to be foretold to the very day, it is wise to adopt a note of caution where spirit timing is concerned. Their idea of 'soon' may be six months or a year ahead!

This is perhaps a good point at which to make clear the difference between a medium and a psychic. Strictly speaking, a medium is chiefly concerned with the spirit world. As I have said, it is my task merely to pass on what I receive from the spirits and this may or may not include guidance for the sitter. A psychic, on the other hand, does not rely upon the spirits for information, although many psychics are aware that they have guides with them who assist in their work.

Psychics may use tarot cards, palmistry, a crystal ball or a number of other means of divination, but they use their clairvoyant and intuitive abilities to interpret what they see. All these methods are skilled arts, and genuine practitioners, whether they are dealing with the future or with issues in the present, should be treated with seriousness and respect. A frivolous attitude, treating a sitting with a medium in the same way as a quick session with an end-of-pier fortune-teller, will produce the response it deserves. I get impatient with the sort of people whose only reason for coming to see me is to ask, 'Can you find out from my Uncle Fred if I am going to win the lottery?'

## GUIDANCE IN EVERYDAY LIFE

Should we expect the spirits to concern themselves with our every-day lives? Since they are living on a higher plane, are they likely to be bothered about material things? These questions worry some sitters. My own view is that, because our spirit friends love us, they care very much about every aspect of our happiness and well-being. They are not very far away. They understand the problems and difficulties with which we have to contend and their hearts go out to us when we are suffering.

I know that some mediums say we should not ask questions of the spirits in sittings, but should be content to accept whatever they give. I personally disagree with this. I always allow time, towards the end of the session, for the sitters to put any questions they wish. I warn them that I may not be able to obtain answers in every case, but I believe that the spirits themselves welcome an opportunity when they can perhaps get across to me some information that they have been unable to convey before. In fact, if the sitting has gone well, the sitter's questions will already have been answered along the way.

'It's easy for you,' people often say to me. 'All you have to do is ask your guides and they take care of everything for you.' I wish it was that simple! I have my share of worries and problems just like anyone else. There are things I have to learn and to overcome. My guides can't live my life for me or remove all the obstacles from my path. But because of the work I do, I have a special relationship with them. I know they are there to help me and that I can trust and rely upon them implicitly.

Some mediums say that they cannot get guidance for themselves, and this too I disagree with. If it involves an issue with which I am emotionally involved, it is difficult for me to be sufficiently detached to receive a clear reply. But I do send a thought 'upstairs' whenever I need help, and I always receive it. I may have to wait a while and the answer does not necessarily come directly in the form of words dropped into my mind. But somehow I will just know what to do, or else the situation will resolve itself, usually in some quite unexpected way, which shows that an invisible influence has been at work.

I do not bother the guides about trivial things which I am well able to work out for myself, but I would not dream of taking any major decision without consulting them. This does not mean that I have handed over control of my life. I know that I am free to accept or reject their advice. But I have learned through long experience that they are invariably right. I seek their guidance, especially if I want to know the best way to help a particular person or the correct way of handling a situation where someone else is concerned. They can look into the hearts and minds of others in a way that I cannot and can see far better than I can the wisest course of action.

Future events are seldom predicted to me, although my move to the country was predicted two years before it happened, by a medium who told me that I would have a house that was on the edge of countryside but just outside a town. My mother, who was a keen gardener, added that it would have a large garden, which I doubted at the time since I had no interest in gardening. However, the spirits were right on both counts – and I often wish I had my mother's green fingers when looking at the overgrown flower beds outside my window!

I am occasionally given warnings which I do well to heed. For instance, some three or four years ago I developed a bad cough. For a long time I delayed going to the doctor, despite an increasingly strong voice in my head warning me that I ought to do so. It will get better of its own accord, I thought. But it didn't and eventually I was forced to seek medical help. By that time, because my chest is my weak point where health is concerned, the condition has become so serious that it needed prolonged treatment, including a stay in hospital. All this I could have avoided had I heeded the warning.

When I asked my guides about it I was told, 'It was not part of the plan for you to become so ill.' So that is an interesting reflection on the question of free will versus predestination. It was, perhaps, inevitable that I should become ill, but because I rejected the advice that was offered to me I suffered more than was necessary. Now I listen carefully to everything and do as I am told!

## SPIRIT HELP AND PROTECTION

It is not only mediums who can receive this sort of loving care. All those who are on a spiritual pathway of whatever kind, who are seeking to find their own truth and to live for the good of others and the earth we live on, will automatically attract to themselves guides who will look after them. As much as is possible within the spiritual laws, these guides will smooth your pathway, help you in times of difficulty and shield you from danger. But they cannot do this if you are not attuned to them. And this is where it is up to you, by prayer and meditation, to build your link with the spiritual dimension.

I have heard many stories which illustrate this spirit care and intervention. For example, a man received a prompting to cancel his flight on a plane – and the plane crashed. And a friend of mine was saved from a serious road accident when an inner voice told her not to move forward at the traffic lights although they had turned green. She sat there and waited while car horns honked behind her. A few seconds later a lorry came out of a side turning. If she had proceeded, her car would have been hit.

A similar story was told to me by David.

In 1982 our first child was born and, like all proud dads, I pushed her in a pushchair wherever we went. We have a crossing on the main road, controlled by traffic lights, where we used to go to the shops. On one occasion my wife was pushing the baby and we stopped at the lights. The lights turned red and a lorry stopped close to the kerb and the traffic stopped on the far side of the road. When the green signal to cross appeared I started to walk in front of the lorry. As I stepped out from the lorry into the second lane an invisible hand pulled me back by the collar. A car going very fast shot across the road and kept going. If that hand had not pulled me back I would have been killed. All those present just sat there with their mouths open and one driver said, 'Who pulled you back?' 'My guardian angel,' I replied.

In seeking the help of guides, as with all aspects of spirit communication, it is motive that is important. If you are spiritually motivated and have love in your heart for others, that love will return to you in the form of guidance and protection. Hardships and problems may come. None of us can escape life's lessons. But if we are attuned to the spiritual dimension and are striving towards spiritual goals, our guides will walk beside us every step of the way.

## ADVICE ON SEEKING GUIDANCE THROUGH A MEDIUM

Before making an appointment to see a medium think carefully. What are your motives? Are you asking the spirits to break any spiritual law in giving you this guidance or information? And is it really a medium you need? If you want psychological insights into a situation or you want to know what might happen in the future, you might be better off consulting an astrologer or a tarot reader. If the problem is an emotional one, consider whether you would benefit more from seeing an alternative therapist of some kind.

If you do decide to see a medium:
- find someone you can trust to be reliable.
- bear in mind that no medium is infallible.
- weigh up carefully anything you are told.
- remember, in the end you must make your own decisions.
- try to keep a clear, detached mind.
- do not 'will' the medium to give you a particular answer.
- wait until the medium has finished before you ask any questions.
- accept that you may not necessarily receive the answers you want!

As well as having a sitting, use your meditation time to seek help from your guides directly, in the following way.

### SEEKING GUIDANCE FROM YOUR GUIDES

Light a candle before you begin. Do the Progressive Relaxation exercise (see page 25) then start your meditation. Formulate your question clearly in your mind and ask it, either inwardly or aloud. Your guides will know your question already but putting in into words will help to clarify your thinking. *Then dismiss the question from your mind.* This is important. Do not dwell on it with your conscious mind. Go into meditation as deeply as you can until you reach that still centre of your being where all is peace.

Be attentive of any words or promptings that come to you, either from your guides or from your higher self. If nothing comes at this time do not be disappointed or strain for an answer. Give thanks as if your request had been granted, end your meditation, blow out the candle and close down and ground yourself as usual (see page 28).

Continue to be attentive for the next few days. The answer may pop into your mind at some time when you are relaxed and not expecting it. You may suddenly just 'know' how to resolve the situation, or things may work out for you in a way you could not have anticipated.

The more you get into the habit of seeking guidance in this fashion, the more easily you will be able to receive it. And the more you give out love and kindness to others, the more you will be looked after in return.

# CHAPTER 7

# Guides and Channelling

A question I am often asked by sitters is, 'Can you tell me about my guides?' So at this point I would like to say a little more about what is meant by guides, how we can become aware of them and how they help us in our spiritual development.

As I have already explained, I was conscious of my guides long before I was conscious of any other spirits, although at that time I was of course not familiar with the term 'guides'. The loving presences who surrounded me were my friends, my comforters, my protectors in a world that often felt alien. When I became involved in Spiritualism I heard mediums talking about their guides, who always seemed to be Native American Indians or Chinamen, or members of some other exotic and ancient race. I was told I too had various guides with me: the inevitable Indian, a Tibetan monk, a nun, a geisha girl, even an Eskimo! I didn't know how many types of guide there were but it seemed to me that I had a complete set.

All this left me confused and not at all convinced. The nun I could accept because I had seen her in my meditation and felt her gentle personality. But why should a Tibetan monk or a geisha girl who may have lived centuries ago have attached themselves to me? My confusion prompted me to ask my guides, 'Who are you? What do you look like?' Strange though it may seem, I had never thought to ask these questions before. The answers came in a series of dreams and meditations. The nun was the first to speak to me. She gave the name of Maria and told me that she had been a nursing sister in France in the nineteenth century. She was still concerned with healing and she had come to help me in this aspect of my work. Another guide appeared to my inner vision in the form of a Greek philosopher. He told me that his function was to give me the wisdom that I was to pass on to others. A particularly powerful guide at that time presented himself as an Egyptian. He held ancient occult knowledge and was there to awaken my psychic faculties, those faculties which I had first developed in an Egyptian life.

There were others whose dress and appearance were more modern and ordinary. They included a man who had been a music teacher and a woman who had worked as a medium during the Second World War. They made no claim to have been famous and did not disclose their names. I never did see an Eskimo, and I strongly suspect that someone's imagination must have been working overtime there!

## THE ROLE OF GUIDES IN MEDIUMSHIP

When I started sitting in my development circle I got to know my guides better. I learned to recognise their individual voices and personalities. I was able to have long discussions with them on the nature of the spirit world and the purpose of existence. I was also aware of the guides belonging to the other members of the circle. Sometimes I could describe their appearance. At other times there was just an impression of a being robed in white. Always they brought great love, like kindly teachers watching over their pupils with tolerance and concern.

There were a number of Native American Indians and Chinamen among the guides, but I came to recognise these 'costumes' as being to some extent an illusion. Guides are for the most part communicating from a dimension where they no longer retain human form. They assume certain forms and personalities in order that we can recognise and identify them. As they have probably lived many times on earth, the appearance they take on will be that of the lifetime they consider most appropriate. In some cases it represents a life in which they and their medium were together. The Greek philosopher told me that he chose to appear in that way because we had shared a lifetime in ancient Greece.

When I see guides now, whether my own or other people's, I am more likely to perceive them in the form simply of beings of light or energies. If asked to describe their appearance, I can only say that I sense an aura of white light.

Certain types of guides are associated with certain qualities. The Native American Indians traditionally associated with mediums represent a race that has natural psychic abilities, a closeness to nature and respect for all living things – all very relevant to the New Age. Chinese guides are bringers of wisdom and often possess an understanding of natural herbs and healing. Monks and nuns represent prayer and devotion and bring a particularly soft, compassionate energy. They, too, are often concerned with healing. Bishops and priests bestow spiritual authority and give inspiration in public speaking. This is, of course, a very general classification. Guides are as individual as we are and they each have their own special gifts and aptitudes which they convey through the medium with whom they are working.

Some of a medium's guides, what I call the 'inner circle', will have been with her all her life, like my own close spirit companions of whose presence I was aware as a child. Others come because they want to assist in the work of communication, having chosen to serve the earth in this way and been specially trained for this. There will also be guides who are there for a particular purpose such as healing or channelling. They are less closely linked with the medium and may only be with her for a short period, or may come only when they are needed to fulfil a specific purpose.

It is unusual for a medium's guides to be anyone she has known on earth though this can happen occasionally. Friends and relatives who were very spiritual people may return in this role. An example is Janine, Julie's daughter, who was mentioned earlier. Because of the progress she has made in the spirit world, Janine now acts as a guide to Julie, helping in her mother's spiritual work. But at the same time, Julie still recognises her as the loving friend and daughter to whom she was so close. However, generally speaking, guides are beings who have moved further along the path of progress than spirit friends and relatives. They are not perfect or all-knowing but they have reached a degree of wisdom that fits them for the task of leadership and teaching.

A medium could not function without the help and co-operation of her guides. They are responsible for the development of her psychic ability. At the same time that the medium is working on herself, meditating and attuning her mind, the guides are working on her, heightening her awareness and making her inner senses more acute. In fact, it is useless for a person to decide that they are going to be a medium if that is not the pathway they are meant to follow. No matter how hard they try it simply won't happen because the guides are not doing what is necessary from their side for the faculty to unfold. This explains why some people sit in development groups for years and never succeed in becoming mediums.

While the medium is communicating with the spirits the guides are doing their part behind the scenes, aiding her in every way. I have spoken of the force field they build up in the room where the sitting is to take place. They harmonise the medium's vibrations with those of the spirit communicators and help those who are unused to communicating to get through. They decide who should be allowed to communicate and bring those people forward so that they are within the range of the medium's perception. Without this organising and assisting, all the spirits would be trying to get through at once and the medium's mind would be swamped with impressions which she would find very hard to sort out.

Every medium also has a 'door-keeper', a guide whose function it is to protect her from disturbance or intrusion by unwanted spirits. The door-keeper may decide that a particular spirit should not be allowed to communicate, or that the medium should not work on that occasion, perhaps because she is over-tired or unwell or because it is not an appropriate time for her sitter to be attempting to make contact with the spirit world. When this happens to me, as it does to every medium occasionally, it is as though the door has been barred and, try as I might, nothing will come through. Fortunately, this is a very rare occurrence and, frustrating though it is, I have to accept that it is always for a good reason.

When I am taking a church service or giving a sitting, as well as trying to be attentive to any mental pictures or sensory impression I am picking up, I am listening intently all the time to the voices I hear in my mind. These may come from the sitter's spirit people, but often it is my guides who are giving me the words I have to pass on. I cannot say at any time which particular one of my guides is speaking, but I do not find it important to be aware of this. I simply attend to the collective voice from 'upstairs' which I know, provided I hear it clearly, is always reliable and accurate.

## THE WIDER ROLE OF GUIDES

All people on earth have a spirit assigned to look after them, traditionally called a guardian angel. This is our closest guide, the one who will always be with us. But all of us who seek to walk a spiritual path – not just mediums and healers – attract a number of guides, whether or not we are conscious of them. These guides help us to unfold our spirituality in every way. They support us in our prayer and meditation and teach us through our intuition and our inner vision. They are with us in any acts of kindness we do to others. But they recognise how difficult our lives can be and they can, when necessary, supply very practical help and advice with material problems. They also assist us in creative endeavours. Many writers, musicians and artists are inspired, knowingly or unknowingly, by spirit helpers.

I rely upon my guides to a great extent in my writing. In fact, without them my books would never see the light of day. They do not do the work for me. I have to use my own mind, carry out any research and bring my own thoughts and ideas to the project. But the initial impulse comes from them and theirs is the guiding hand that steers the book from its inception to completion.

I start my working day with about half an hour of meditation, during which time I attune to my guides and ask them to work with me. I then wait until the words begin to drop into my mind, and only then do I begin. Sometimes, I have to admit, I get impatient and try to start without them. The result is usually a frustrating morning, a headache and an overflowing waste paper bin! But if I am properly tuned in the words will flow and the ideas will be expressed more skilfully than they would be if I were working alone. This is very typical of the way in which guides co-operate with us. They do not do our work for us; rather, they help us to bring out the best in ourselves and to use our own natural abilities to the full.

The following visualisation will help you to become conscious of the guide who walks with you.

### ATTUNING TO YOUR GUIDE

Open as usual by relaxing and saying a prayer. Take a few minutes to centre yourself and still your mind. Then visualise a golden light above your head. With each breath you take, you are being drawn up into that light. You are rising up above your body ... floating high up into the air, leaving the world behind. You feel totally relaxed and as free as air. You are in the clouds, floating ... floating ... Now you see a scene beginning to form before you. You are in the countryside. All is peace and tranquillity. The grass at your feet is soft and green. There are wild flowers of many colours. In the distance are gently rolling hills. There is a soft light that permeates everything but does not hurt your eyes. In front of you there is a tall tree, its leaves swaying in the slight breeze. Under the tree there is an old stone bench. Go over to the bench and sit down. In a few moments your guide will come and sit beside you. (Pause for a couple of minutes.)

Your guide is sitting beside you now. What does he or she look like? Are you given a name? Sense the energy of your guide ... feel their love and concern for you. Picture the light that radiates from this person. Listen to any words they may speak. Do not strain your mind ... just rest in this loving companionship, knowing that you and your guide are as one. Your minds and souls are merging … you are completely at one … completely at peace. (Pause for five or ten minutes.)

Now it is time to come back. But before you go, your guide puts a gift into your hand. Look at it … and take this gift with you as you say goodbye to your companion. Walk back across the grass. You float up into the air … you are floating … floating … back into the room … into your body. Now open your eyes.

Recall the gift that was placed into your hands. Think about its symbolic meaning for you. This may give you some insight into the nature of your own gifts or your spiritual pathway.

## DEVELOPING YOUR CONTACT WITH YOUR GUIDE

The first time you try the above exercise you may see nothing at all, but persevere. Your guide will definitely be there even though it may take you a while to perceive this. You may just get a sense of your guide's personality. This is really all you need. What you are developing is a soul to soul contact that goes beyond words and images.

Doubts may come into your mind – *Is this just my imagination?* We all have these doubts when we start. And yes, the imagination can produce images and fantasies. The way to overcome this is by regular practice. Each time you meditate, ask your guide to make him- or herself known to you. In time you will come to recognise their energy. Another doubt that troubles many people who begin linking with their guides in this way is, 'How do I know that I am contacting a true guide of light?'

It is only sensible to be cautious about this. Just as there are impostors in this world, so there are spirits who, though they are not evil, attach themselves to people who are vain and deluded. These are false guides, and they can cause a lot of confusion and do a great deal of harm by giving untrue and misleading information. So how can you tell the difference?

True guides of light will come with love and wisdom. They do not make extravagant claims about themselves so be very wary of any guide who claims to be a famous personage. Genuine beings of light will not try to take over your life, demand that you obey them unconditionally, or say or do anything that diminishes you. Rather, they will bring you strength to fulfil yourself and invite you to co-operate with them in a partnership. They will not flatter you or promise you wonderful spiritual gifts, but will gently point out when you are doing something wrong and support you with encouragement. Very often they display a delightful sense of humour.

You should ask yourself how you feel while the guide is with you. Do you like the energy you sense? Does it feel warm and loving? When you have finished your meditation, do you feel uplifted or drained? A true guide will bring you energy, not deplete you. If you are not completely happy with what you feel, challenge the guide by asking if he or she is of the light. Should you receive no reply, or should you sense anything that makes you at all uncomfortable, ask for protection, finish your meditation and close down.

When developing any form of channelling or mediumship, it is important to keep a balance in your life and not get carried away by enthusiasm. Humility is also important. If you allow yourself to become egotistical your discernment is impaired. You can then easily be deceived by your imagination and become vulnerable to the influence of false guides. I have known channellers who started out with the best of intentions but, because they allowed their ego to get in the way, their contact with spirit became distorted and out of balance. They began to develop exaggerated ideas about themselves and to lose touch with reality, eventually growing disillusioned when their former followers turned away from them.

However, provided that you are sincere and motivated by love and you keep this vital balance and humility, you will not encounter anything other than true and loving beings. According to the spiritual law, like attracts like. If you are seeking in sincerity, that of itself will give you protection. The higher you raise your consciousness, through prayer and meditation, the more evolved will be the guides you draw to you.

Once you have established contact with your guides you need to build the link by regular meditation. Call on them in your thoughts each time you meditate. When you feel a response, hold that link steady. Sense the thoughts and the love passing along the bridge of communication from you to them and back again. Absorb the energy they are transmitting. Let yourself be filled and energised by it.

When we are getting to know friends on earth we take pleasure in talking to them, learning about their lives and finding out their views and opinions. So do the same with your guides. Talk to them in your mind. Ask any questions that occur to you. Sometimes you may get an immediate response. At other times you will have to wait for answers. They may be dropped into your mind a few days later or they may come through a book you read or something someone says. But one way or another, the answers will be given.

It takes time to build this bond, but once it is established you will know that you have companions who are constantly at your side and will be with you throughout your life – and beyond.

## CHANNELLING

Another way of building and maintaining a link with your guide is through channelling. The word 'channelling' was coined in America, where it is often used as a more modern word for 'mediumship'. There is, however, a slight difference. Mediumship is associated with the communication with deceased loved ones and has its historical roots in the Spiritualist movement which started in the nineteenth century. Channelling is very much a New Age phenomenon. A channeller is more concerned with contacting guides and other entities, sometimes to give personal guidance but more often to receive spiritual teaching. This may come not only from guides but also from within the channeller's own being.

When I was starting my work as a medium, channelling was very much in fashion in America. The rich and fashion-conscious had their own private channellers whom they consulted as avidly as, a few years before, they had consulted their analysts. Like many British mediums, I regarded this new craze with suspicion. Most of the so-called 'channelled' material I had read, imported in large quantities from the USA, seemed vacuous and uninspired. The beings with whom channellers claimed to be in touch were diverse and sometimes quite bizarre. They included not only guides but angels and archangels, exalted personages such as Jesus and the Virgin Mary, devas, nature spirits and extraterrestrials. It seemed to me that there was endless scope here for self-delusion and wishful thinking. My mind boggled at the ETs, who didn't seem to have anything particularly original to say beyond admonitions to save the planet and live in brotherhood, and it hardly needed a being from another dimension to tell us that.

Then one day someone gave me a brochure for the School of Channelling in Worcestershire. I read it and my curiosity was stirred. An inner prompting told me that this was something I really should investigate, so I booked myself in for a channelling course. Rather to my surprise, the course turned out to be an important step forward in the development of my mediumship, showing me a slightly different way of working with my guides that was to prove of great value.

Runnings Park, where the School of Channelling is based, is a centre for health, healing and self-development. It is located in one of the most beautiful parts of England, the Malvern Hills. There is, as I discovered, a very special energy about this place. The deep peace and the breathtaking views are certainly conducive to meditation and the spirit world felt very close to me there. There were eight participants on my course. I was the only medium though all the others had some previous experience of channelling and psychic development. The group was led by the director of Runnings Park, Tony Neate, who founded the School of Channelling in 1992.

We were taken through a series of exercises designed to teach us how to attune to our guides in such a way that they could speak through us. This was subtly different from the way in which I had been trained to attune in the development circle and the way in which I usually worked. Instead of receiving the impressions from a spirit and passing these on, this technique taught me to go into a meditative state, ask the guide for inspiration and let the words flow without conscious intervention.

That should have been easy for a medium to do, but in fact I found it very difficult. I could hear the words forming in my mind, but as soon as I opened my mouth to speak they vanished completely! I was relieved to find that other members of the group had the same difficulty, which is a common problem when starting out in channelling. It became easier when I was told that I didn't need to go into a deep trance, just to make a small shift into a slightly altered state of consciousness. This, in Spiritualist terms, is what is called 'overshadowing'. It is not a form of possession nor is the medium taken over or controlled by the guides. It is a state in which the guides blend their consciousness with that of the medium, who then speaks the words they put into her mind.

After a couple of days of practice I found this state easier to achieve. I never lost consciousness but I felt as if I was slipping further and further away. Though I could hear the words coming through me, it wasn't me speaking them. The more I learned to let go and trust the process, the more the guides could take over. The sensation was a very pleasant one. I felt suspended in a deep peace where nothing else mattered. The world seemed very far away. I never wanted to come back to ordinary reality. When I did come back, I felt slightly disorientated for a couple of minutes although it did not take me long to recover. But the spiritual energy with which I had been filled had a soft healing quality that remained with me for a long time afterwards.

If I had been asked who was speaking through me I couldn't

have said. Sometimes I recognised the familiar vibration of one of my inner circle of guides, but sometimes the communicator was unfamiliar to me. Yet I knew I was safe and protected and that whoever came was coming in love. It didn't seem important to have a name or an identity and this is one of the main differences between mediumship and channelling. In mediumship, great emphasis is placed upon establishing the identity of the communicator. In channelling the source of the material is not of paramount importance, provided that what comes through seems to the channellers and the listeners to be true and good.

When the course was over I continued channelling and incorporated this technique into my work. I use it when it seems appropriate in sittings, as a means of allowing the sitter's guide to speak to them directly. The information that comes through at these times is always very significant to the recipient. It has a special quality that goes straight to the heart. I also use it for teaching in small groups, when a guide will come through and give teaching. I too am often surprised to hear the words that come out of my mouth, which are expressed with a depth of compassion and understanding and are frequently very moving. I have sometimes opened my eyes to see half the group in tears, not of sorrow but of emotion, because the love that envelops the whole room is so deep and beautiful.

The great advantage of channelling is that you don't have to be a medium to do it. You do, however, need to be self-disciplined and honest with yourself in evaluating the communication you receive. There is no need to go into a deep trance. When channelling started most channellers did work in this way, but over the years this has changed and most channellers today work in a light trance or a slightly altered state of consciousness in which they are aware of the words that are being spoken through them.

I would recommend anyone who wishes to learn to channel to attend a course at a centre such as Runnings Park, or at least to study one of the numerous books now available on the subject (a couple of titles are included in Further Reading). To develop channelling you need the help of a partner or you can practise within a group. At every session one person should be appointed to remain detached and to direct the session and keep a record of everything that transpires.

### CHANNELLING YOUR GUIDE

Sit opposite your partner. Relax and centre. Say a prayer asking for protection to be put around both of you. Send out your thoughts to your guides asking that you may be used as a channel. Then wait patiently, keeping your mind as still as possible.

If the guide who draws close to you is one with whom you are already familiar you should not find it too difficult to attune to him. If you feel the approach of a guide you do not know, it may take you a while to align your mind with his vibration. If you are at all nervous or uncomfortable with what you are feeling, ask the guide if he is of the light. The response should be a warm, loving feeling. If you do not receive this, bring yourself back to full waking consciousness and bring the session to a close. As I have said, provided that you are working in love and sincerity you are most unlikely to encounter any being who is not of the light, but if you are unfamiliar with this method of communication your mind can give rise to nervousness or apprehension. Your guide will understand this and will withdraw until you are ready to try again.

Assuming that all is well and you wish to proceed, as your guide comes close focus your mind on what you are receiving and be alert for any words that come to you. You may feel yourself slipping into a trance-like state but you are unlikely to lose consciousness completely. Generally, you need only be in a slightly altered state of consciousness, though finding the right level does require a certain amount of practice. My guides describe it to me as finding the point of balance. If you don't go deep enough you cannot hold the link. If you go too deep you cannot get the words out.

Once you find that point of balance, the words will begin to flow. This is where you have to learn to trust. Try not to anticipate what is being said or to edit the words in any way. Let them flow through you. You may well find that although you can hear what is being said, you can remember only snatches of it afterwards, so it is helpful to record the session and listen to it later. You may surprise yourself when you play back the recording and hear what you said.

Alternatively, have a pen and paper with you and write down any words that come into your mind. Some people find it easier to channel through writing than by speaking aloud. When the flow of words has stopped, finish the session and close down and ground yourself in the usual way.

## ASSESSING CHANNELLING MATERIAL

Because of the nature of channelling, it can be difficult to assess the value of channelled material. This is a problem that I as a medium am very much aware of. All forms of mediumship need to be carefully evaluated, but traditional forms are easier to judge. When you are dealing with communications from departed men and women who give information about themselves, it is possible to check the accuracy of this information and thus decide whether or not the medium is really in touch with the person to whom she claims to be speaking. This does not mean that everything that particular medium says will be reliable, but it does provide some yardstick by which to judge. With channelling, both the person doing the channelling and the listeners have to use their own intuition and sensitivity to decide whether or not to believe what is said.

Channellers often have doubts about their own ability. 'Is it me?' they ask. It is hard to give a straightforward answer to this because the channeller's mind does play some part. When a person is channelling, the guides do not take over completely as if the channeller were an empty vessel whose vocal cords they manipulate like a puppet. As I have explained, it would be more accurate to describe channelling as a blending of minds, with the guide influencing the mind of the channeller so she will speak his words. But this spiritual contact cannot help but activate her subconscious mind, which lends its own colouring to what comes through. Much of the skill in channelling lies in learning to raise one's level of consciousness so as to receive and repeat the guide's words without distortion or colouring, but such eventualities can never be completely discounted.

In assessing the value of what you receive through channelling, you need to ask yourself the same questions I listed for assessing communications received from a guide. Were you comfortable with the vibration of the guide? How did it make you feel? You should also look carefully at the words you have spoken (and, hopefully, recorded). Did what was said ring true to you? Was it given in a loving, supportive way? Did it go beyond your own conscious knowledge? Was it expressed better than you could have expressed it yourself?

If you are on the receiving end of channelling you should ask yourself these same questions. It is also helpful to consider whether the channeller seems a sensible and well-balanced person and whether – without expecting her to be a saint – her life reflects the general tenor of her teaching. Caution is especially needed in assessing some of the more extreme claims of channellers who say that they are in touch with beings such as Ascended Masters or ETs. Whether or not this is the case is open to question. What one person finds acceptable will be implausible or even ridiculous to another. But the New Age is all about personal responsibility, thinking for ourselves and making our own judgements. I always like to keep an open mind. Even in apparently outlandish claims there may be some truth. A channeller who claims to be in touch with Jesus, for instance, may be linking into the cosmic or Christ consciousness, which is the highest form of energy it is possible to contact, even though her guide is not the historical Jesus.

It is sometimes said that channelling does no harm, even when it emanates from the medium's subconscious, but on this point I have reservations. If channelling consists, as much of it does, of no more than platitudes and injunctions to live a spiritual life, this may be harmless enough. But channelling can be extremely dangerous to gullible people who lack the discernment to distinguish true from false. Great harm can be done by those channellers who take it upon themselves to give clients advice about their personal lives – advice that can be disastrously wrong.

Channelling does, however, when practised sincerely and well, bring great benefits. It gives you a closer contact with your guides. It can be a means of gaining inspiration for writing, painting, music or any creative art. It also brings you closer to your own higher self, which is your own wisdom and the deepest, most wonderful part of your being. In opening yourself as a channel you connect with the light and energy of the spirit world and anchor this energy in our world, for the development of your own spirit and to bring light to those around you.

CHAPTER 8

# *Healing Energy*

Spiritual healing is one of the most precious of gifts. Like mediumship, it is a form of channelling, with the healer acting as a channel for the universal healing energy. Many mediums also work as healers. The great value of spiritual healing is that it works on every level, emotionally and spiritually as well as physically. For this reason it has been called 'the therapy that reaches the parts other therapies cannot reach'!

## MY INTRODUCTION TO HEALING

I was introduced to healing through Spiritualism. On my first visit to a Spiritualist church I noticed after the service a small group of people sitting in a room at the back, apparently waiting for someone. I was told that they were waiting to have healing, though they looked fit enough to me. As I watched, a man and a woman went into the room. After a few words of greeting, they invited the people in turn to sit on the stools placed in the middle of the room. The healers then placed their hands gently on the patients' heads and appeared to go into a state of meditation. I was asked if I would like to have some healing but, as I was perfectly well and in any case wasn't sure about this strange ritual, I declined.

It wasn't until quite some time later that I decided to give it a go. I was suffering from a particularly bad bout of hay fever that was making my nose run and my eyes water. I wasn't sure that healing could help me, but I reasoned that at least it couldn't do any harm, so I duly presented myself at one of the church's healing sessions. I was asked to sit on a stool. Two healers came to attend to me. One stood behind me, the other sat in front of me holding my hands. The one standing behind me said a prayer, then gently laid his hands first on the top of my head and then on my forehead and my throat. I was conscious of a sensation of warmth and relaxation spreading through me. Almost miraculously, the head-ache and stuffiness began to lift.

The healing session only lasted about five minutes, but after-wards I felt so much better – and not only physically. My spirits were lifted and I felt refreshed in every way and charged with energy. Sadly, the cure was not permanent. The hay fever came back, as the healers had warned me that it might. But I had several days' relief, and when it did return it was never as bad again.

This incident occurred when I was just starting to develop as a medium. I was told that I, too, had the potential to be a healer if I chose to direct my energies in this way. This presented me with a dilemma. I thought that it would be wonderful to be able to help people, not just with minor ailments such as I had been suffering from but with more serious complaints, but I simply didn't have time to pursue two avenues at once. As usual, I asked 'upstairs' for guidance.

'You are to be a medium,' I was told. 'That was what you came here to do. But you will heal in your own way.'

And so it has proved to be. Although I am not a professional healer, I do occasionally give healing when people come for sittings. But the healing that is channelled through me operates more often on a mental and spiritual level than on a physical level. It assists in alleviating tension and stress and makes it easier for the sitter to be receptive to the spirit world. In a sense, I see the whole of my work as a form of healing, in that it helps to alleviate suffering, brings peace of mind and guides people to find their inner knowledge of spirit.

## HOW HEALING WORKS

Spiritual healing has existed for thousands of years. The Egyptians and Greeks practised it. It was used at the time of Christ, who himself performed healing miracles. In the last few years healing has gained in popularity, due to the tremendous surge of interest in alternative therapies of all kinds. After many years of being regarded as a fringe medicine, healing has become quite respectable. In Britain it is now officially listed as a therapy recognised by the National Health Service, and doctors are permitted by the General Medical Council to refer patients to healers. Many doctors and nurses have a natural healing ability and some are now recognising this fact and are practising openly.

Healing has been part of the belief and practice of Spiritualism almost since the Spiritualist movement began in the middle of the nineteenth century, and has always been regarded as an important feature of its ministry. All Spiritualist churches offer healing free of charge. Some Anglican and Roman Catholic churches now also have healing groups. In addition, there are hundreds of healing sanctuaries and healers who practise in their own homes.

In recent years scientists have begun to take this form of therapy seriously and have conducted many studies which have proved it to be effective. These experiments have demonstrated the many ways in which healing is beneficial. For instance, it has been shown to strengthen the immune system, the body's defence against disease, and to bring about relaxation and peace of mind. It can also speed up the healing of wounds. It alleviates the side effects of chemotherapy and other painful forms of treatment. In laboratory tests, healers were able to arrest the growth of cancer cells. Even plants germinate more quickly when healing energy is applied to them. The American Dr Daniel Bendor, who has investigated this subject for ten years, says in his book *Healing Research*, 'If spiritual healing were a drug, they'd have put it on the market long ago.'

Healing starts from the premise that man consists of a number of different bodies that interpenetrate. Of these, the physical body is the most dense. Next comes the etheric body. This links our physical being to the higher bodies – the astral, mental and spiritual. Our health and well-being depend upon the harmonious flowing of the life force within these subtle bodies. This life force is a universal energy. In Hinduism it is called 'prana'; in the East it is known as 'ch'i'.

We take in ch'i through the food we eat and the air we breathe, but we also absorb it at the more subtle levels of mind and spirit. Ch'i enters at the etheric level, where it is stored, and from there it is transmitted, through the chakras or energy centres, to every part of our being. When there is an adequate flow of ch'i we feel strong and well. However, sometimes the flow becomes blocked or out of balance. These disruptions to the energy flow begin in the mind, with stress and fatigue, or with negative emotions such as fear, hatred, anger and resentment. Over a period of time they manifest in the physical body in the form of sickness or disease. The flow of ch'i in the body can be likened to water flowing through a river. Wherever there is an obstruction the current is disturbed. Silt and debris accumulate at these points and eventually pollute the water.

Healing starts at the point where illness starts, at the etheric level. Healers attune themselves to the universal healing source, then, like a channel or conduit, transmit the energy to the patient. At this point the patient's own innate self-healing ability takes over, absorbing the ch'i and directing it, through the etheric body and the chakras, to wherever it is needed, removing blockages and restoring balance and harmony.

Spiritual healing should not be confused with faith healing. The latter, by definition, depends upon the patient having faith in the healer. Spiritual healers do not ask patients to believe in them. The energy they use is not their own, but is channelled from the divine source. Nor do they diagnose the cause of an illness, although they may well sense what the problem is or know instinctively whereabouts in the body the patient is experiencing pain. A medium's job is to channel communications from the spirits to the sitter, whereas the healer's job is to transmit the healing energy and leave the rest to the patient's inner self.

Healing is effective even when the person to whom it is being directed does not know that the healing is being sent. For this reason, healing can be used to treat babies, patients who are unconscious or too ill to ask for help, or those who do not understand its benefits. It is suitable for animals as well as people, and animal healing has become very popular in recent years. Animals in fact respond very well and seem to know when the healer is trying to help them.

However, healing is not a miracle cure, even though sometimes the effect can be dramatic. There are many cases on record where patients who had been given up by conventional doctors have recovered, leaving the medical profession baffled. But usually the results are less dramatic. Patients may need a number of sessions, especially if the illness is serious or deep-seated. Even then, healing does not necessarily bring about a complete cure. But patients almost invariably feel some response: an improved ability to relax, an increase in vitality and a lightening of the spirits.

It is important to remember that healing is not a substitute for conventional medicine. If you are receiving medical treatment you should continue to follow your doctor's instructions and not leave off any medication without prior consultation. Healing works well with orthodox medicine and with any form of complementary therapy, bringing about a swifter and more complete recovery.

I know from my own experience how valuable healing can be. The worst period of illness I have had in my life was caused by the serious chest condition I mentioned earlier (about which I unwisely disregarded my guide's advice). If possible I have always avoided taking any kind of drugs, but sometimes they are necessary. On this occasion I was put on a course of strong antibiotics, which had the unpleasant side effect of making me feel sick and depressed. A very dear friend of mine who is a healer came round to see me and was horrified at how ill I looked. She got to work on me straightaway. As soon as she laid her hands on me I felt the strength flowing into my body. I subsequently had healing many times, from her and from other friends, until I was better. My cure was undoubtedly achieved through the medication and the skill of the doctors (without which I would not be here today writing this book), but the healing was a vital adjunct. Coming when I was at my lowest ebb, it was the turning point. It gave me the will to pull myself together and fight the illness and restored my cheerfulness and optimism.

However, you don't need to be physically ill to seek healing. When you are tired or run down, it is because your ch'i energy is low. A dose of healing is just what is needed at these times to recharge the batteries and get you up and running again. I now have healing whenever I feel tired or depleted. I regard it as a tonic, better than anything I can buy in a bottle! I am deeply grateful to the many healers who have helped me in various ways over the years, and I have to say that they have been some of the kindest, most spiritual people I have ever met. Many of them work devotedly, year in and year out, for no payment or reward except the joy of helping people through their gift. In many cases they have come to healing having suffered themselves in some way through illness or bereavement, and this enables them to empathise with others.

## WORKING AS A HEALER

The qualities needed to be a healer are similar to those needed to be a medium: patience, compassion, and the willingness to make yourself as clear a channel as possible for the energy that flows through you. I think, however, that healing calls for more selfless devotion. Healers don't always have the satisfaction of the instant feedback that a medium gets from sitters. Whereas a medium usually sees a sitter only once or at long intervals, a healer may work with a particular patient for weeks or even months. And sometimes the healing works at such a subtle, non-physical level that patients may not appreciate how much they have been helped and changed by it.

When there is no obvious cure, healers, being the responsible, kind-hearted people that they are, tend to blame themselves. One of the things they have to learn is to preserve a professional detachment, as doctors and nurses have to do. There are many reasons why a patient may not respond to treatment. For instance, the person may be unconsciously holding on to his illness because he needs it as a prop, a way of winning sympathy or a means of avoiding issues in his life he does not want to face. The illness may be a karmic one, resulting from past-life conditions. If the patient knows, at a deep soul level, that he needs to undergo this particular test because there is something he has to learn from it, then no amount of effort on the part of the healer will remove the illness. What healing will do, however, is give the patient help and strength to carry the burden.

It is hard for a healer when a patient dies. Healers often take this very much to heart and feel that they have failed in some way or that they did not do enough. Here again, they should not blame themselves. If it is a person's time to pass into the spirit world, then healing will not cure that person. Healing is, however, of great benefit to terminally ill patients. It alleviates pain and gives a better quality of life. I know of many cases where a patient who had been receiving healing lived far beyond the period of time predicted by the doctors. And when they did die, they passed away peacefully and painlessly.

## HEALING GUIDES

Spiritual healing is not the preserve of any church or religion. As the energy upon which it draws is universal, so this therapy transcends all boundaries of race and religion. Not all spiritual healers are Spiritualists, although many are. And many healers are aware of the guides who work with them. These guides may have been doctors or healers when they were on earth and are now continuing their mission in the spirit world. They work in partnership with healers, as they do with mediums. A healer attunes to the guides, who blend their energies with hers, and together they transmit these energies to the patient.

The presence of the guides is sometimes so strong as to be

almost tangible, as I found out a few years ago when I was having healing from a friend. I often used to feel heat emanating from her hands but on this occasion it was so intense that I exclaimed to her, 'Your hands are so hot on my shoulders.' To my surprise, she told me that her hands were not on my shoulders. And, turning round, I saw that she was standing a little way behind me. It was her guide's hands I could feel, bringing a comforting touch.

As I have mentioned, the guide who mainly helps me with my healing is a French nun who had worked within a healing order. It is her I call upon whenever I give healing to a sitter, although I am aware that there are other guides in the background also assisting. I always start by saying a prayer and asking for a blessing upon the patient. At this point I feel her come very close to me and overshadow me. It is as if I am enfolded in her robe. As I place my hands upon the patient's head I feel a great wave of compassion flow through me into the patient. My hands tingle and become very hot. Sometimes I feel compelled to place my hands upon the part of the body where the problem is. At other times I will hold my hands a short distance away from the patient. Because the healing works at the etheric level there is in fact no need for physical touch.

I continue with the healing for as long as I feel the energy flowing. This may be just a few minutes or a quarter of an hour, seldom longer. When it stops I know that my guides have done all they can. I then end by giving thanks. Finally, as patients will have opened up psychically during the healing, I place a protection round them by visualising their chakras closing and the aura sealed with a golden light.

## FINDING A HEALER AND HAVING HEALING

Healing is not the main part of my work, so if I feel sitters would benefit from a course of this therapy I advise them to find a suitable healer. Always choose a healer with great care. Just as there are good and bad mediums, there are good and bad healers. If possible, seek a personal recommendation or go along to your local Spiritualist church where healing will usually be available. Alternatively, get in touch with a recognised healing organisation (see Useful Addresses). Ask about the healer's experience and qualifications. Also ask about fees. Though most healers give their services free, some work on a professional basis and make a moderate charge. This should be in line with the fees of any alternative health practitioner. Avoid any healer who makes exorbitant charges or who promises to perform miracles.

The procedure for healing is very simple. The healer will ask you to sit on a stool or chair or you may be invited to lie on a healing couch. There is no need to undress. He or she will then place their hands gently on your head, shoulders or back. Sometimes you may experience a sensation of heat or tingling. At other times you may not feel anything at all, but this does not mean that the healing is not working. Relax and try to open your mind and make yourself receptive to the power that is coming through. The session may last a few minutes or may take up to half an hour. When it is over remember to thank the guides as well as the healer for what you have received. Then close down as you would do after meditating.

Depending upon the severity of the condition, you may need to see the healer a number of times. During this time you should do all you can to help yourself, both physically and mentally. We are all ultimately responsible for our own health. It would be pointless consulting a healer for a stomach-ache, for instance, if you continued to eat the foods that upset you. Similarly, if you do not try to let go of the negative emotions that are at the root of your health problem, it will not go away. Even if a healer succeeds in treating your immediate symptoms, they will re-emerge later in some other form.

Like a sitting with a medium, a healing session works most successfully when there is harmony between the healer and the patient. If after a time you feel you are receiving no benefit, it may be that you and that particular healer are just not on the same wavelength and the healer is therefore unable to make an energetic link with you. This does occasionally happen, and it is no one's fault. Find another healer with whom you feel more in tune.

Should you be ill, don't wait until things reach a crisis state before seeking healing. Obviously, when illness develops you should first consult a doctor and take any advice and medication prescribed. But have healing as well; this way it has a better chance of working and can perhaps prevent the condition from becoming serious. Bear the same thing in mind with your pets when they are receiving veterinary care. They too will benefit from healing.

## BECOMING A HEALER

The basis of all healing is love and compassion. If you send out loving thoughts to people in need, or if, as a parent, you give a child that has hurt itself a hug to 'kiss it better', you are already giving out healing energy. However, to work professionally as a healer it is advisable to undergo a period of training with a recognised body (see Appendix and Useful Addresses). Avoid any course that offers to make you into a healer in the space of a weekend! Like any psychic skill, becoming a good healer requires time, patience and dedication.

Reiki healing has become very popular in recent years. Reiki originated in Japan in the late nineteenth century and is now recognised world-wide. It is similar to spiritual healing in that it is a system for transmitting subtle energy. There are some excellent Reiki healers around, but again take care when selecting one. Sadly, Reiki has been exploited by so-called 'masters' who charge large sums of money to 'initiate' pupils in the art. While it is reasonable to make some charge for any course of instruction, such blatant commercialism is contrary to the whole spirit of healing, which should be motivated by sincerity and the wish to serve.

Even if you are not a qualified healer, you can safely give

healing provided you remember certain basic rules. Always work in love and sincerity. Attune yourself to the highest spiritual level you can, in order that the energy channelled through you will be pure. Do not seek to impose your own ideas on patients or 'will' them to get better. It may be that their illness is a karmic one that their higher self has chosen and from which they are learning a valuable lesson. Ask only that the healing that is received is used in a way that is for the patient's highest good. Do not diagnose or prescribe treatment – this should be left to the doctors. And do not attempt to give healing when you are tired or unwell. Energy always flows from a higher to a lower level. If you are depleted you may do your patients more harm than good because you will be drawing energy from them rather than the other way round.

### GIVING SPIRITUAL HEALING

Sit your patient on a stool or chair and stand behind him. Take a few deep breaths until you feel calm and at peace. Still your mind and lift your consciousness so that you become filled with love and light. Say a prayer asking simply that you may be a channel for the healing energy. Send out your thoughts to your healing guides, asking them to link with you so that you may work together. Try to sense them drawing close. Take as long as you need over this. It is important to be properly attuned before you begin.

When you feel still and centred, visualise a golden light above your head. Feel this light coming down into you through the crown of your head, down to your heart and flowing into your hands. Then place your hands gently on the patient's head. At this point you may feel a sensation of heat or tingling in your hands. The patient may feel this also. If you feel guided to do so, move your hands gently over the patient's shoulders and back, or wherever you feel directed. The guides know where the need is and will direct you to move your hands accordingly. Often, it is enough to stand quite still, without even touching the patient but just letting the energy flow.

When you feel the flow 'switch off', bring the session to an end. To do this, visualise the patient's chakras closing and mentally surround him with golden light, sealing the aura. Then step back from your patient, mentally detaching yourself so that you do not absorb his conditions. Close yourself down in the same way, making sure that both you and your patient are thoroughly grounded.

## DISTANT HEALING

One of the most remarkable things about healing is that it can work perfectly well even when the healer and patient are not physically together. Many healers offer an 'absent' or 'distant' healing service, and a number of healing organisations have lists recording the names of people for whom healing is requested. This is particularly useful for people who do not have a healer in their area who can visit them in person, or for people who are housebound and unable to find a healer to call on them at home. It also means that patients can receive healing very frequently – daily, in the case of serious illness – by having their names put down on a number of healing lists.

Healing sent in this way can be beneficial even if the recipients do not know that the power is being directed to them. This, incidentally, demonstrates that healing is a powerful force and does not depend upon a patient's faith in it. But when patients are aware that healing is being sent, and consciously attune their minds to receive it, the effect is more marked.

There have been occasions when I have been unable to visit a healer in person, so I have arranged with them a time when I will sit quietly at home and they will transmit the healing to me. When this is done, I invariably feel a wave of love and energy. Sometimes I have suddenly found myself feeling better for no apparent reason and, on phoning one of my healer friends, have been told, 'That was when I was sending you healing!'

For sceptics who find it hard to believe in healing at all, the claim that energy can operate over any distance will seem absurd. Such is the case, however. The power of thought has no limits. Patients who have been thousands of miles away from their healers have reported cures. This form of healing doesn't only help individuals. Healing sent out to trouble-spots in the world, places where there is war and suffering, will help to bring light into these situations.

## SENDING DISTANT HEALING

For those who wish to give some form of service on a spiritual level but do not know how, distant healing is an excellent way to start. Anyone can do it – it requires no special knowledge or gifts. I send distant healing every day. Although it is not essential, I keep a book in which I list the names of anyone to whom I wish to direct the energy, and I suggest this as a useful memory aid.

A good time to send healing is at the end of your regular meditation period. (I hope by now you are meditating regularly!) While you still feel attuned to spirit, ask your guides to work with you in this way. You may be aware of a particular guide who comes in answer to this request. Think of each person you know who is in need of healing or go through the names listed in your healing book. Say each name aloud or, if you prefer, in your mind. If you know what these people look like, visualise them. *But do not focus your mind on their illness.* It is very important to remember this or you will be sending negative rather than positive energy. Picture them as being happy, healthy and full of vitality.

You don't have to spend a lot of time over this. A brief, but sincere thought for each person is enough, asking that they be helped in the way that is best for them. You do not even need to know anything about the people concerned, so you might like to invite your friends and family to add names to the list. Remember also that the list can include people who are troubled mentally or emotionally, since the healing will help them to cope with the problems. You can send healing to animals as well. And don't forget a thought for any parts of the world where there is suffering.

When you have finished your healing, give thanks for the energy that has been given then close down from your meditation and ground yourself in the usual way. You have done your part. Know that your guides will now use the love and the power you have sent out and will direct it to wherever it is needed.

You may feel when you begin distant healing that you are not having any effect, but wait and trust that it does work. Your patients will soon start to tell you how they have benefited. And you will find, incidentally, that by seeking in this way to help others your spiritual awareness will increase. According to spiritual law, whenever we give service to others, we receive blessings in return.

Jack Angelo, in *Your Healing Power*, says, 'When you link, in love, to the light that is everywhere – healing must follow.' Healing, in its deepest meaning, is all about helping people to find the light within them so that they can be cleansed and made whole. As many people these days are discovering, it is a beautiful energy to receive and to work with. It helps us to increase our own light and to connect with the spiritual essence that is at the heart of our being.

# CHAPTER 9

# Coping with Sensitivity

Being a medium brings many rewards. But in order to do this work I have to be highly sensitive, which can cause problems in terms of health, vitality and dealing with the demands of every-day life. These problems are experienced by a great many mediums, psychics and healers. They frequently begin in childhood.

## MEDIUMSHIP IN CHILDHOOD

I have already mentioned how quiet and withdrawn I was when I was very young. This withdrawal, which used to worry my family, was my means of escaping into my own world where all was peace and harmony. The outer world seemed so harsh. I was born with an unusually thin skin. Any criticism I took seriously to heart. If there was a disagreement between my parents it was useless for them to try and hide it from me because I could sense it in the air. If someone around me was depressed or in a bad mood I detected it and it made me edgy and uncomfortable. Raised voices – even if they were not directed at me – made me want to run away and hide.

I don't want to give the impression that I was mistreated or neglected as a child. Far from it. I had a secure and loving family who did everything they could to make me happy. It wasn't their fault if sometimes I couldn't respond to their affection, or if they couldn't tell what was in my mind. No one could enter my inner world, which I shared only with my spirit companions.

My sensitivity made my years at primary school difficult. I knew I was different in some way from the other children and I found it hard to join in their games. This was something the other children sensed, and though I was never bullied – it was quite a genteel school, run by two elderly spinsters – I was made to feel an outsider. This difficulty continued, to an extent, when I went on to secondary school, although by then I was better at mixing with people and I had many friends. Academically, I did quite well. I was naturally studious and loved books. It was no hardship to me to work well and do my homework. Some of the teachers, however, terrified me. Teachers were much stricter in those days. Though I excelled at English, a look from the English mistress, Miss Kennedy, would reduce me to a quivering jelly. As for answering back – the thought would never have entered my head!

Physically, I was never very robust. Every winter during my primary school I missed weeks of term through coughs, colds and other infections. My health improved as I got older, but even when I was well I was never one of those children with boundless energy, and I needed plenty of rest and quiet.

By the time I had grown up and left school I had learned to conceal my sensitivity under an outward veneer of self-confidence. I had also learned to toughen up a little, not to make myself hard or unfeeling but to protect myself against the world. I enjoyed going out to work, learning new skills and meeting new people, but I never lost the feeling I had had for as long as I could remember, of being somehow different and not quite belonging.

When I became involved in Spiritualism I was comforted to discover that many mediums understood and shared my feelings. I was struck by how many of them described their childhood as unhappy and said they had felt different and alienated. Like me, they had been shy and timid, adversely affected by things other, more robust, children took in their stride such as starting at school, mixing with other children, tension in the family and parental disapproval. Many of them had been sickly or had suffered a major health crisis during their early years.

A few had had parents who understood them and even saw their sensitivity as a special gift to be encouraged. They were the lucky ones. Most were labelled odd or were thought to be excessively shy. This was not so bad for the girls but it was particularly hard for the boys, whose fathers thought they were wimps because they wanted to be indoors reading a book instead of out playing football with the lads.

Of course, it is not only those who grow up to be psychics who have these difficulties in childhood. Many children are highly sensitive. Because of this they are often misunderstood by their parents and do not receive as much attention or approval as their more outgoing siblings. Consequently, they have low self-esteem and feel that they are flawed in some way.

## PROBLEMS CONNECTED WITH SENSITIVITY

Sensitive people, with their natural warmth and kindness and intense sympathy for others, are often attracted to work in the caring professions as doctors, nurses, therapists or counsellors. But while they feel a need to give out help and healing, their sensitivity may make it hard for them to cope with many aspects of their own lives. I see this paradox in so many of the people who come to me for sittings.

Relationships are often problematical for sensitive people. They tend to be easily hurt and over-react to any real or imagined hurts and slights. Women – and sometimes men – complain that their partners don't share their beliefs and aspirations. With couples, this arises particularly when one person opens up to spiritual things and begins to change as a result, while the other remains unsympathetic or even begins to question the sanity of that person. Friendships, too, can suffer when people become more spiritually aware. They now find that they are on a different wavelength and old friends may drop away. I lost a number of friends when I began working as a medium. Some of the people I had known for years suddenly didn't want to keep in touch with me any more, though I made many new friends with whom I was in harmony.

Sensitive people sometimes get stuck in unsatisfactory relationships because their deeply felt sympathy for others makes them reluctant to do anything that would hurt their partner's feelings. They will put up with all sorts of unkind and inconsiderate behaviour, making excuses like 'I know he doesn't mean it. I know he's a good person inside.' They know that there is good in everyone, if only it could be brought out. 'If I could just get him to open up to his spiritual side,' they lament, 'then things would be different.' But the longed for opening may never happen and meanwhile they continue to be unhappy, put upon or even abused. Often, too, these kind-hearted souls attract partners who are emotionally weak and needy and, in caring for them, they neglect their own needs.

Another complaint I often hear is 'He [or she] doesn't give me any space!' This need for space is felt by all psychics and sensitive people. They desperately need a place they can call their own, even if it is just a tiny box room, and time when they can be completely undisturbed. These periods of solitude are absolutely essential to find inner peace and allow jangled nerves to recover. Unfortunately, shutting yourself away can be very difficult if you have a demanding family, and to a less sensitive partner such action can come across as coldness or withdrawal.

But the problem that is complained about more than any other is depletion and lack of energy. I so often hear the cry, 'I'm always so tired. What am I doing wrong?'

All sensitive people need plenty of rest. Their auras are more delicate than the average person's and therefore their energy becomes depleted more quickly. Even walking through a crowded street can leave them tired because the people they pass who are themselves depleted will draw off a little of their vitality. Healers and therapists have a particular problem in this respect. They are constantly dealing with people who are needy in some way and, because of their concern to help, they are apt to give away too much of their energy without replenishing themselves. If this continues for too long, the result is burn-out and exhaustion. And as their energy levels drop, it becomes harder to prevent even more energy being drained away – and at the same time their resistance to illness and infection is lowered.

Many sensitive people radiate healing energy quite unknowingly. Anyone in their vicinity who is unwell subconsciously detects this and is drawn to them like a magnet.

'Complete strangers come up to me and tell me their problems,' sitters sometimes tell me. This is one of the signs which tell me that a person has healing potential. However, people like this can easily 'pick up' the health conditions of those with whom they come into contact. Unless they are alert to this danger they may not realise that it is not *their* depression, headache, sore throat or whatever it is that they are feeling.

## PSYCHIC GIFTS AND HEIGHTENED SENSITIVITY

Being psychic and being sensitive go hand in hand. Sensitive people have a natural, instinctive awareness of the spiritual side of life. The material things are not enough for them. They need to develop their spirituality and can never feel fulfilled unless they do so. But should they choose to develop as mediums, channellers or psychics they may encounter further difficulties. For when you begin to expand your psychic awareness, your sensitivity increases on every other level as well.

I discovered this to my cost when I began sitting in a development circle. Physically, I noticed that I tired even more quickly than usual. I became nervous and jumpy. Loud noises hurt my eyes. Visits to the cinema, which I had previously enjoyed, became uncomfortable because of the high volume of sound and the flashing lights. Doing a stressful office job became almost impossible. Travelling on crowded rush hour trains drained me even before I arrived, and sitting at a typewriter all day left me completely exhausted.

Emotionally, too, I was becoming more vulnerable. I was

experiencing mood swings that couldn't be accounted for by normal hormonal changes. One moment I would be in the depths of despondency and the next, as if a switch had been thrown, I would feel elated. I was more easily moved by the plight of those who were suffering. Watching some disaster on the news could have me in tears. Sometimes I felt 'spaced out' and 'not quite there'. There were other times when my nerves were so jangled that I just had to go away somewhere and be on my own until I felt better.

Though I didn't realise it at the time, all these effects were caused by the fact that I had allowed myself to become too open psychically and was not properly grounded. The importance of closing down and grounding had been explained to me in my development circle but I had failed to realise just how vital this was. When you are caught up in the excitement of feeling your psychic gifts unfold it is all too easy to get carried away and to neglect other areas of your life.

Today, I still have to guard against becoming psychically depleted. Being a medium is very demanding, to say nothing of writing books, keeping up with a large volume of correspondence and running a home, and there are times when I have to cancel everything and allow myself a good rest. But I have learned over the years how to conserve and balance my energies.

## KEEPING YOURSELF IN BALANCE

If you are developing your psychic ability, or if you are a sensitive person, you need to keep a good balance in your life. Sensitive people tend to live so much in the mind and the spirit that they neglect the physical side of their being. Recognise that you may not be as physically robust as other people and do not push yourself beyond your limits. Nurture your body by having a good, wholesome diet, eating organic food wherever possible. Consider whether you might need a vitamin and mineral supplement. Have spiritual healing whenever you feel you need it or treat yourself to a massage or an aromatherapy session. There is no reason why you should not be as healthy as anyone else, but a little extra vigilance is needed to recognise and deal with the symptoms of over-exertion.

Be kind to yourself. Looking after yourself and considering your own needs is not selfish. If you are not well and happy, how can you support or be of help to anyone else? However busy you are, make space every day when you can meditate. If possible, arrange holidays where you get away from everything for a while. This is especially important if you work from home and the phone is always ringing. Even if you can't do this, take time out frequently to listen to music, go round the shops, walk the dog or do whatever you enjoy that is just for you. If you're anything like me you hate noisy parties, but an evening in the company of like-minded friends will leave you feeling on top of the world again.

When you relax, make sure you relax completely. Collapsing in front of the television is not enough! Relax the mind as well as the body. Push aside those troublesome thoughts that chase each other round your brain – things you must do, things you have for-gotten to do, the demands of other people. The world can do without you for a few minutes! Insist on having some time alone, whether your family understand this need or not.

Make time for your hobbies. One of my main relaxations is music. When I was young I learned to play the piano. I now have an electronic keyboard which gives me hours of pleasure. I also find singing very therapeutic. Singing, incidentally, is very good for developing the throat chakra, which governs clairaudience. Animals I also love, though, not having a pet of my own at present, I have to 'borrow' a cat from a friend!

Keeping yourself grounded is very important. Your spiritual energy needs to be supported with the physical energy drawn from the earth and absorbed through the lower chakras. If a person focuses too much on the spiritual and neglects the material, the lower chakras do not open sufficiently. This leads to weakness of the physical body and lack of vitality. In this state it is easy to sink into depression and despondency and lose the joy of life. Even psychic gifts such as mediumship cannot operate properly in a person who is ungrounded. It requires the energy of the lower chakras to 'boost' the medium's awareness to the spirit dimension.

The simplest way to ground yourself is to be with nature: walking in the open air, working in the garden. When you do this, try to feel a real connection with Mother Earth. Sense her energy rising up through your feet and legs and filling your whole being. I am not a gardener but I like to get out into the countryside or walk in the park as often as I can. I never cease to feel a lifting of the spirits when I see the wonder and beauty of creation.

Any form of physical movement is good for grounding. If you are not the sporty type, doing a little exercise at home, even something as simple as swinging your arms, dancing or deep breathing, is remarkably effective in getting your energy going and restoring vitality. Whatever you do, you need to bring your attention fully down into the body. Love and appreciate your body as the wonderful temple it is. Some psychics live so much in the head that they see their bodies merely as something to keep their heads from bumping on the ground!

## THE IMPORTANCE OF CLOSING DOWN

If you are constantly tired and you cannot discover the reason, or if you find yourself being depleted by other people, it is probably because you are too open psychically. All psychics, and all sensitive people, should learn how to close down their chakras. I gave a brief exercise for closing down in Chapter 2, but as this is such an important point I want to look at it in more detail here.

We all have within the aura a psychic web which protects us from intrusion both from the astral plane and from the thought emanations of those around us. This is a necessary defence mechanism. Without it, we would constantly be picking up impressions from the spirits and from everyone we came into contact with. When your spiritual awareness is heightened this web becomes sensitised and is more easily permeated. This makes you more vulnerable on a psychic and emotional level and makes it harder to seal the aura.

In many sensitive people the solar plexus centre particularly is too open. This comes from their natural sympathy for others, and the problem is very prevalent among healers. When a person feels compassion for someone in need their energy flows out to that person through the solar plexus centre. The needy person soaks up the energy like a sponge and, without any intention to do so, may drain the healer of more energy than can be spared. Healers often continue thinking about a patient after the session has finished. In accordance with the occult law that says energy follows thought, all the while they are doing this, their energy is flowing out. Like doctors and nurses, they need to develop a professional detachment, giving care and sympathy to patients when they are with them but, at the end of the session, leaving the work to the guides or the universal healing energy – and to the patients' own responsibility. It is not a healer's duty to try to heal the world!

In mediumship the problem is slightly different. When someone is working as a medium the psychic web is constantly being stretched in the effort to reach out to make contact with the spirits. When the medium closes down it contracts again. However, if the medium overworks her gift, particular if she tries to work when she is ill or under stress, the web becomes damaged like a piece of elastic that has been pulled and pulled and can no longer go back into shape. The throat and brow chakras that are used in mediumship can also become over-strained until the medium reaches the point where it is hard to shut off the awareness of the spirit world in order to attend to everyday life. In some cases, spiritual healing is needed to repair the damage.

The following exercise is helpful for mediums, healers and those engaged in therapy but anyone who is sensitive should use it regularly in order to close down and ground their energies. It is a slightly more complicated version of the simple closing down exercise given in Chapter 2.

## CLOSING DOWN AND GROUNDING EXERCISE

Sit quietly and take a few deep breaths. Be aware of the floor beneath your feet. Then try to sense the earth itself, its power and stability. Imagine that you have roots going down from your feet extending deep into the earth. Let all your tension drain away through those roots into the solid ground.

Take a deep breath and draw the earth energy up into the soles of your feet. Feel it spread up your legs and travel through your whole body, filling every cell with vitality. Take it right up to the crown chakra at the top of your head. Now visualise a golden light above your head. See this light cascading all over you like a waterfall. Take it in through the crown of your head and feel it descend through each of the chakras, starting with the brow and the throat then on down to the heart, the solar plexus, the sacral centre and finally the root chakra, visualising each one closing like a flower. Pay particular attention to the solar plexus. You might like to picture here a shield or a cross, fixed firmly in front of you.

Take the light right down to your feet then let it travel on down into the earth. Then bring the light up again, through the chakras once more, closing each one at the back. As you do this you should feel a slight contraction in the aura. When the light reaches the crown chakra feel it spreading out and wrapping itself around your whole aura, enclosing you in an egg of golden light. This light will seal the energy within you and shield you from any negativity.

You should do this exercise whenever you have been meditating, healing or working psychically in any way, or even if you have been thinking or talking about psychic things. Always do it before you go into crowded places or if you have to deal with stressful situations or have to confront people who you know will draw upon your energy.

# FLOWER ESSENCES

Another aid that I have found extremely helpful in restoring balance and energising myself is flower essences. The Bach flower remedies, which were developed by Dr Edward Bach in the 1930s, are widely known but in recent years there has been a huge growth in the production of other flower essences produced by the same method.

I am fortunate in living not far from The Living Tree, in Milland, Hampshire, which is the biggest importer and distributor of essences in Britain. They have a bewildering array, including the very popular Australian bush flower essences, the Alaskan flower and gem essences, Himalayan flower enhancers, Araretama rainforest essences and the Goddess remedies that are produced in Canada. There is now even a range of animal essences (no animals are harmed in their manufacture).

All these essences work at an extremely subtle level and are very suitable for people who are sensitive. They are useful for a whole range of conditions: physical, emotional and spiritual. My particular favourites are the Himalayan flower enhancers. These, as the name implies, are designed not to focus on problems but rather to enhance what is right within our being, supporting growth and spiritual development. Each one of the enhancers vibrates at the rate of the particular chakra for which it is intended. By taking a few drops, the chakra is brought back into balance.

# POSITIVE ASPECTS OF BEING PSYCHIC

I have dwelt at length on the negative aspects of being psychic but, of course, there is a positive side too. For me, the greatest advantage it brings is knowing that I am surrounded by loving spirit friends whose care of me never fails. I have been greatly comforted at times of bereavement by knowing that the person I loved was no more than a thought away, in a happier world. I also value the guidance that comes to me whenever I need it and the support I receive whenever I have to face pains or difficulties. This gives me a sense of security and a confidence that nothing can take away from me.

Having a highly developed intuition also has its advantages. I won't say that I can read a person like a book – and despite what some people think, I can't read minds – but I do have an instinctive sense of who is to be trusted and who is sincere and I go by this more than by outward appearances. I follow my promptings, even when they seem to go against reason and common sense. This helps me not only in major areas of my life but in minor things. The other day, for instance, I felt a prompting to go to the library although I hadn't intended to go there, and a book I had long been searching for, and which I had never seen in there before, was sitting on the shelf waiting for me.

Little incidents like this are what I consider the perks of the job. But, most of all, I value my gift as a means of fulfilling my purpose for this incarnation. It gives me the privilege of helping others along their spiritual pathway and sharing the knowledge of the world of spirit that is so close to our own world.

## SELF-HEALING VISUALISATION

As well as seeking to heal others, you can use your spiritual awareness to heal yourself, through meditation or guided visualisation. This is one of my favourite visualisations. You may like to burn some aromatherapy oil – sandalwood and frankincense are good for meditation – and have some quiet music playing in the background.

Lie on a bed or on the floor and relax completely using the Progressive Relaxation technique. Feel all the stress and tension draining away into the earth. Then let the scene unfold before your inner vision.

You are standing in a pine forest. It is cool and dim. The trees are straight and tall, their branches reaching up high into the sky. There are patches of dappled sunlight on the path in front of you. Walk slowly down the path. Hear the twigs crackling under your feet ... see the little creatures as they scamper about ... smell the fragrance of the pines. As you walk along you come to a clearing. In the clearing is a temple. It is built of pure white marble. Two white columns flank the door, which is approached by a short flight of steps. Go up the steps, feeling the cold marble beneath your feet. The door stands ajar ... push it open and go inside.

The light in the temple is soft. The walls are pale blue. In the ceiling above your head, there is a skylight through which you can see the clear blue sky. In the centre of the temple is a low healing couch, draped in blue velvet. Walk over to the couch ... lie down on it. You are completely comfortable and relaxed. The healers of the temple come up to the couch. They are clad in blue robes. Their faces shine with love and light. They stand around you. One of them places his hands gently upon your head. You feel the healing energy stream from his hands and from all the spirit healers. The energy is pouring down into you, recharging, revitalising you. Relax and absorb the love and the healing. (Pause for about five minutes.)

You now feel fully recharged and healed. Get up from the couch. Thank the healers for their care. Walk back to the door, closing it behind you. Return, taking the path through the pine wood. Bring yourself back into the room, into your body. When you are fully back, sit up and do the Closing Down and Grounding exercise.

Your temple is your own special place. You can return to it whenever you are in need of healing and revitalising. You can always meet your healing guides there, feel their love and blessing and draw upon the universal source of all love and healing to replenish body, mind and spirit.

# CHAPTER 10

# Running a Home Circle

I n recent years I have noticed a great increase in the number of small spiritual circles and groups meeting in people's homes. This is another sign of the growing New Age consciousness that is so prevalent today. More and more people are seeking. They are not attracted to churches and religious institutions but they want somewhere where they can go to meet others of like mind, meditate, learn and share experiences. These informal meeting places are the answer, and they can be immensely valuable. The loving energy that is generated uplifts all the members and helps them to increase their spiritual awareness more successfully than they could on their own.

Running groups like this has become a major part of my work and it is something I very much enjoy. It gives me great pleasure to bring people together and watch them growing and developing and to be able to pass on what I have learned through my experiences. But you don't need to be a medium or a psychic to run a group. I would like to explain how you can run one in your home and how, in doing this, you will be creating a sanctuary, a place of power that will benefit not only you and the group members but all those who come within its walls.

## SETTING UP A GROUP

If you would like to start a group, there are a number of things you need to consider. Obviously, the first question is who you are going to invite. You don't need a lot of people. An ideal number would be seven or eight, but what matters is the enthusiasm of the members and whether they are willing to make a commitment to attend regularly. In this respect, even two or three people who are dedicated and sincere is better than a large number who just turn up when they feel like it.

It is a good idea to have a preliminary meeting, to make sure that your chosen participants are in harmony with each other. It is not enough that they are friends or can get along with each other socially. There needs to be a deeply felt spiritual harmony. Unless everyone is on the same wavelength and shares the same basic beliefs and aims the group will not gel. At this meeting you will, of course, need to decide where and how often you are going to meet. Once a week is usual. Any less frequently and it is hard to keep the continuity going. I am assuming that you will want the meetings to take place in your home. It is best to always use the same place rather than moving round from one member's house to another's, as the energy will be harder to build if you keep changing the venue.

More importantly, this preliminary meeting should be used to discuss fundamental issues. What does each person hope to get out of the group? Have they any relevant knowledge or expertise they can bring to it? What do they hope to achieve? Then you need to decide what the group is going to be for. Is it for meditation or healing or is it for the development of mediumship and channelling? It may be possible to combine some of these as you go along but the group needs a focus of will and intention.

A further point to be settled is who is going to lead the group. As the host, you are the obvious choice, but if there is someone who is more experienced you may wish that person to assume the role. It is possible to take it in turns to conduct the meeting but someone must assume responsibility for the general running and organisation.

It may require more than one meeting to reach agreement on all these points, but this is time well spent. The more you get to know and understand each other before you start, the more harmonious the group will be. Also, during the course of these discussions, you will no doubt be able to tell if there are any members who do not seem suitable for the group, and you can tactfully

point this out to them and save yourself the embarrassment of
having to ask them to leave later on.

## PREPARING THE ROOM

Having settled all these points and set a date for the first meeting,
you now have a very important task – preparing the room that you
are going to use. Ideally, a separate room should be set aside for
this purpose. As soon as my husband and I moved into our present
house, I laid claim to what was formerly the dining room. I do most
of my spiritual work here and it is not used for anything else. Even
the television has been banished! This room has become my
sanctuary. When I meditate on my own I like to sit in here because
I draw strength from the atmosphere of peace and healing.

If you don't have a spare room in your home that you can
reserve for a sanctuary, choose the quietest room rather than
somewhere where there is a lot of activity. To be really thorough,
you should first redecorate it in a suitable soft colour. My own
room is blue, which is a healing colour. Pink is associated with love
and compassion. Green is the colour of balance and harmony, and
gold and violet are the most spiritual colours of the spectrum.

Should redecorating be impracticable, at least give the room a
thorough spring-cleaning, whether it needs it or not. Throw open
the windows, vacuum the carpet, wash the curtains and polish the
furniture. This may seem a chore if, like me, your idea of
housework is a quick flick round with a feather duster, but it is
worth the effort because it will make the room feel so much
brighter and fresher.

In fact, all rooms need cleansing from time to time, on an
etheric as well as a physical level. Negative energy builds up from
everyday living and accumulates in the corners like dust and
cobwebs. When there have been arguments or tension in a room,
or if anyone has been depressed or ill there, the effects linger on
invisibly for a long time.

Various methods can be used to dispel this negative energy.

Burning incense or aromatherapy oils is one good way. Frankincense and sage are traditionally associated with purification. I like the electric oil diffusers that work by applying gentle heat to a pad soaked with oil. These are very cheap to run and can safely be left on for several hours. Alternatively, you can buy Native American Indian bundles of sage called smudge sticks.

There are a number of flower essences that have been specifically designed for cleansing rooms and meeting places. Of these, the ones I particularly like are the Sacred Space Formulas in the Alaskan Flower Essence range (available from the Living Tree, Milland, see Useful Addresses). The Purification formula is for cleansing and purifying one's personal energy field and breaking up stagnant energy. 'Guardian' creates a protective force field, while 'Calling All Angels' is an invocation to the angelic realm.

Sound and movement can also be used to clear stale energy. So put on a tape of lively music, sing, dance or bang on a drum, or whatever makes you feel happy and energised. Then stop, sit quietly and sense how different the room feels.

When you have finished your cleansing you need to furnish the room. The furnishings should be kept simple. A few upright chairs and a small table are all you need. If the room has to be used for other things as well, you may not have the opportunity to refurnish it, but this is not vital. What matters is the thought that you put into it. In most of the houses where I have lived I have had to make do with the living room. No one entering those rooms would have noticed anything strange about them, but strangers coming in would often remark, 'What a lovely atmosphere there is in here!'

One thing you should have in your sanctuary is an amethyst crystal. Amethyst helps in the purification of a room by absorbing negative energy. You should cleanse your crystal from time to time by washing it under running water and leaving it to dry naturally. Fresh flowers give off a good energy so keep some flowers in there all the time. The room should always be kept clean and tidy and you should give it a 'dust and polish', in the psychic sense, before each meeting of the group.

Now that your room is prepared the final thing you have to do is to dedicate it. The act of dedication will place a blessing and protection over your sanctuary and will raise the energy. Your dedication can be as simple or elaborate as you like; it is the intention that is important, not the formula. I used the following ritual to dedicate my sanctuary. You can devise your own, or adapt this one to your own taste.

## DEDICATING A SANCTUARY

Choose a time when you are not going to be disturbed in your room. Light your incense or oil burner and, if you wish, have music playing in the background (soft music this time!). Place a candle on a small table in the centre of the room but do not light it yet.

Take a few minutes to be still and attune yourself to your spirit guides and the spirit within yourself. Then light the candle. As you do so, visualise a beautiful golden white light coming from above and filling the centre of the room. Taking the candle, move slowly round the room, picturing the light spreading out in every direction, penetrating every corner, cleansing and purifying. Feel yourself merging with that light. As you do so, it becomes stronger and brighter.

Say the following prayer or, even better, make up your own. The words are not important as long as the feeling comes from the heart.

I call upon the holy angels of light to bless and protect this sanctuary and all who come within its walls. May each member of this group be guided and inspired to unfold their spiritual gifts and to use these gifts in the service of others. May all that is said and done in this place be in love, truth and harmony.

What you have now created is a sacred space, a place where the veil between heaven and earth is thinner. This place will shed its light over your whole house and your family and will be a meeting place for you and your spirit friends. Honour it and enjoy it.

## RUNNING A GROUP

Once your sanctuary is cleaned and dedicated you are ready for your first meeting. Allow yourself time for the final preparations, so that you are not rushed and flustered. Like a good host, you should make sure the room looks cosy and inviting. Put the chairs out ready and set out a glass of water for each person. Make sure the room is pleasantly warm but not too hot, and that the lighting is soft but not too dim. Perhaps put on some background music and burn some aromatherapy oil. All these things help to set the tone of the evening so that when members come in they will feel that they are entering a sacred space.

When everyone has arrived and taken their places you are ready to begin. At this stage, even though the members of the group will already know each other, there is usually a slightly tense atmosphere. People may be a little nervous and uncomfortable, not sure what to expect. This will soon pass as things settle down, but there are various things you can do at the first meeting to establish a sense of the group as an entity and to blend the energies of everyone present. If you feel ritual to be appropriate, the one given below can be adapted so that everyone can take part.

### OPENING RITUAL

Place in the centre of the table one large candle (unlit), and around it put smaller candles in holders, one for each member of the group. Ask the group to join hands around the table for a few moments. (Don't worry – this is not a seance!) You can then use the prayer of dedication given earlier (substituting 'we' for 'I'). Each person then lights a candle from the large candle in the centre. As they do so they speak a few words from the heart, asking in their own way for a blessing upon the group. They then place their candles back in the holders. Allow a few more moments for everyone to stand in silence, visualising the light growing stronger and brighter until it envelops the whole group.

I always open every meeting of a group with a short prayer. Prayer attracts loving angelic beings. It raises the vibrations of the room so that you can more easily come into attunement with your guides and your own inner self. It is a good idea to take it in turns to say this opening prayer. The shyer members may be reluctant to do this but they should be gently encouraged. Once they have made the initial effort, it is surprising how quickly they gain in confidence and realise that their contribution to the group is just as valuable as that of the more outspoken members.

Care does need to be taken in the wording of prayers in order to respect the beliefs and religious affiliation of each member. Some people are uncomfortable with the word 'God', preferring a term such as The Source or The Creator. A non-Christian may not be able to join in a prayer addressed to Jesus Christ. However, the general concept of Light and the angelic kingdom is one which everyone who sits in a group should find acceptable.

After the prayer, I lead my groups into a meditation. At the first meeting a form of meditation should be used that assists in building up the group energy. The following exercise is one I often use.

### BLENDING THE ENERGIES

The members should sit round in a circle, close enough to link hands comfortably. The leader then gives the visualisation.

Take a few deep breaths and relax completely, then join hands. Close your eyes. Be aware of the energy that is in this room and, on the out-breath, send that energy on a wave of love to the person sitting on your left-hand side. Feel it going out through your hands and fingertips. Sense the power building and flowing clockwise round the group. (Pause.) Now feel it change direction and flow round anti-clockwise. (Pause.)

Take another deep breath and, on the out-breath, feel your aura expand on the left-hand side so that it touches the aura of the person sitting on your left. Now, on the next breath, expand your aura to touch the person on your right. Finally, feel your whole aura filling with light and expanding. Now all your auras are blending in one light, one field of energy. (Pause.) Now drop your hands and rest in the power. (Pause for about five minutes.) When you are ready, in your own time come back and open your eyes.

The group leader should establish a routine for the group, a general formula that is followed each time. The meetings should never be allowed to drift aimlessly. There is nothing more disheartening than sitting staring blankly at each other and asking, 'What shall we do this evening?' You might like to draw up between you a list of suggestions for things you would like to try: different guided visualisations, for instance, or varied forms of meditation. As the group progresses it will take on its own structure and you can change anything you feel isn't working. But there always needs to be some sense of direction, so that you know where you are going and can measure your progress.

From time to time you may wish to invite new members to join you. Be very cautious about this. Once a group is established, a newcomer, however well liked by the rest of the group, may disrupt the energies that your guides have been working so hard to blend and balance. Introduce new people one at a time. If there is someone you think would be suitable, invite them to attend one meeting only, as a guest. This gives the group the opportunity to decide whether the visitor would blend in harmoniously. If it is decided that this person would fit in, then he or she can be asked to join, but if not, no one's feelings are hurt.

Running a group can call for considerable tact. You may think you know the members well, but as time goes on, tensions may surface because sitting in a group heightens sensitivity. This means that small irritations get magnified out of all proportion. Two people who don't really get on but can tolerate each other when the group starts may reach the point where they can't stand the sight of each other. Jealousies can arise if one person thinks that someone else is making more progress or is taking up too much of the group's time and attention.

This sort of friction creates problems for the group leader. Should you try to smooth things over or should the offender be asked to leave? I always put such problems 'upstairs' and ask my guides to sort them out. I usually find that people who do not fit in will leave of their own accord, without my having to ask them. Sometimes, however, the problems are too deep to be resolved. I have seen groups break up because of petty jealousy and clashes of personality. This is a pity because, basically, the people concerned have been sincere and spiritually minded. On the other hand, some groups run for years with never a cross word and the members become closely bonded in friendship. Many of my dearest friendships have been formed in such groups.

At the end of each meeting, the members should 'close down' psychically. I know I keep stressing this, but it is an important point to remember. The group leader should take the members through the closing down procedure set out in Chapter 9. After this, a cup of tea or coffee and biscuits round off the evening and bring everyone firmly back down to earth. This final part of the evening can be just as valuable as anything that has gone before. The spiritual pathway is a lonely road. A successful circle is a support group in which the members learn from each other and help each other to unfold the spirit within.

## TYPES OF GROUPS

Groups can be formed for meditation, for healing, and for the development of psychic and spiritual abilities. Meditation groups are the most common. These are the easiest to set up and run. They require no special knowledge or skill. Everyone can learn to meditate, and in this busy and stressful world in which we live today everyone can benefit from it.

There are great advantages to meditating in a group. Many people find it hard to keep up this practice regularly at home because of lack of time or noise and interruptions from the family. A group provides an oasis of peace and calm, free from distraction. The energy generated builds up a force field in which the consciousness of every member is raised, making it easier to attune to the spiritual dimension.

Since meditation is the first step in any kind of spiritual development, I always include a period in every group meeting for going within and making the mind still. I find that everyone enjoys this. Once a group gets used to sitting together in this way, the deep peace that descends upon the room is so restful that they never want to come back!

In a new group, it is best to start with fairly short periods of meditation. Ten or fifteen minutes is enough to begin with, working up to half an hour or more as you become more experienced. Each meditation should be led, either by the group leader or by the members taking it in turn. The following is an example of a suitable group meditation.

## GROUP MEDITATION

I would like you to make yourself very still and calm. Put aside all the cares and worries of the day. Be aware of the light that is building within this room. Take a deep breath and breathe in this light. Feel it penetrate every cell and atom of your body. As you breathe out, let go of all tension, all anxiety. This period of time is just for you, a time when you can go within and be at peace. Continue to breathe deeply and evenly. With each breath you go deeper and deeper within. Your body is becoming lighter and lighter. You are entering a higher state of consciousness. You are becoming at one with your higher self and with the spirit guides and beings of light. I am now going to leave you for a few minutes to your own private meditation and when it is time I will call you gently back.

Whoever is leading the meditation should not go too deep, as it is
this person's job to keep an eye on the group, to make sure that
everyone remains relaxed and comfortable and that no one is
falling asleep! At the end of the agreed time the meditation should
be brought to a close as follows:

> Take a few deep breaths and, as you do so, feel yourself coming
> back into your normal state of consciousness. Be aware of the
> physical body. Stretch your arms and legs if you wish. Be aware
> of the chair you are sitting in and of the room and when you
> are ready, in your own time open your eyes.

Try experimenting with different forms of meditation. There are
many books available which give suggested methods and exercises.
See what works best for the group. Chanting is particularly good.
The effect of a group of people chanting together for ten or
fifteen minutes is very powerful and generates a wonderful energy.
Guided visualisations are particularly suitable for use within a
group. One person reads the script while the rest watch the images
that arise in their minds.

You can, of course, devise your own visualisations but unless you
have a very fertile imagination, it is probably best to write them out
beforehand, so that they flow smoothly. The nature of the journey
can be anything you wish: a trip in a boat along a peaceful river, a
walk up a mountain, a visit to a temple or a descent into a pyramid.
Read slowly, allowing the listeners time to experience whatever
impressions come to them. Try to describe the scene as vividly as
you can and lead the listeners to a point where they can be left for
a few minutes, to experience whatever it is their inner self wishes
to convey to them.

### A GUIDED VISUALISATION

Relax deeply and focus within as you listen to the sound of my
voice. You are about to go on a journey, a journey of self-
discovery. This journey will take you very deeply into your own

being. Watch the images that arise in your mind's eye. Be alert to any words that come into your mind.

It is night time. All is still and calm. You are in the desert. Above your head is a full moon. The stars are shining brightly … the soft light of the moon lights up the sand dunes that stretch out on every side. You are completely alone but you feel safe and at peace. You are wearing a simple white robe … there are sandals on your feet. As you walk along you feel the sand beneath you. Continue walking, enjoying the peace and the solitude, looking up at the stars.

In the distance you see a pyramid … its white capstone gleams in the moonlight. You feel irresistibly drawn towards it, fascinated by its air of mystery. You approach the pyramid. The rough stone walls are immeasurably ancient. As you walk along the outside you can just make out a small door in the wall. When you touch the door it opens, as if by magic. You step inside the pyramid … it is cool and dark. On the floor just beside the entrance is a lighted lantern. Pick up the lantern. This will guide you on your journey.

Before you is a flight of steps … they are steep and narrow. Holding the lantern, you start to go down the steps … down and down … deeper and deeper, into the very heart of the pyramid. At the bottom of the stairs is a low archway. Light is coming through this archway. It is so low that you have to stoop to get under it. Go through the archway. You find yourself standing in a round chamber. Above your head is a high vaulted ceiling. The light is so bright in here that you no longer need the lantern so put it down on the floor. You become aware that the light is emanating from a figure that stands before you. It is an angel. The angel is beautiful, tall and majestic and radiating love and compassion. Look into the angel's face … gaze into the eyes. The angel seems strangely familiar to you, like someone you knew long ago but have forgotten.

The angel has a message for you. What is the angel telling you? Listen carefully … the message may come as words or it may be a picture or a symbol. It speaks to your deepest being, bringing wisdom and inspiration. Receive the angel's message. (Pause for about ten minutes.)

The angel comes very close to you ... its light surrounds you. You and the angel are merging, becoming one. The angel's light is your light ... the angel's wisdom is your wisdom. The angel is your own higher self. It is what you truly are, your eternal self.

Now, slowly, the walls of the chamber are dissolving. The angel fades away ... but you are filled with the radiant light and energy transmitted to you by the angel. Take a few deep breaths ... bring yourself back into the body. Stretch your arms and legs ... come back into the room ... and in your own time open your eyes.

The visualisation now forms a basis for discussion as everyone describes their angel and talks about what they experienced.

## DEVELOPMENT CIRCLES

If you wish to develop mediumship within a group, it is best to have an experienced medium to lead you. The medium will be able to teach you the methods used to attune to the spirit world, assess your progress and help you sort out the difference between spirit communication and impressions that arise from your imagination, always a tricky field for newcomers. However, if you feel you have the potential for mediumship and there is no medium available to assist you, it is still possible to develop the gift within your group. You can obtain much useful help and advice from the Institute of Spiritualist Mediums (see Useful Addresses) through their Home Circles Link.

In order to build the awareness of spirit, each member of the group should meditate for a period of time every day. It is also helpful to make a regular practice of the Candle Meditation given in Chapter 2. When you come together in the group, start with a short period of meditation so that everyone can relax, go within and still themselves. After this there can be a brief time for discussion in which the members can share any experiences or insights they have received.

The next stage is to attune your minds to spirit. To do this you once again have to make the mind still. But this time, instead of focusing within yourself, send your thoughts outwards in order to link with the spirit communicators. You have to actively create a bridge of communication with them. The following exercise, which should be led by the group leader, will assist you to do this.

### CONTACTING THE SPIRITS

You are now going to raise your consciousness so as to attune your mind to those loving spirit beings who are gathering around us. Take a deep breath and feel the energy of the earth beneath your feet. Breathe in that energy so that it comes up through the soles of your feet into your ankles and legs. The energy now reaches the root chakra at the base of the spine. Feel a gentle warmth at the base of the spine. Feel the energy rising up the spine. It is now entering the solar plexus chakra. Feel the solar plexus centre gently expanding. With each breath the energy ascends higher and higher. Now it is reaching the heart chakra. Feel the heart chakra expanding. The energy comes into the throat chakra, through which we gain the ability to hear the voices of spirit. It now reaches the level of the third eye, which is the centre of clairvoyance. The spirit world is all around us, no more than a thought away. You are a spirit being and can be aware of the spirit people.

Feel the brow centre opening like an eye. Send a concentrated beam of power out from this centre, reaching out to connect with the world of spirit. Hold your attention steady on this beam of power. Feel your perception expanding. The spirit people are drawing close to you along this bridge of communication. Talk to them, call them closer. Be alert for any impressions that are coming into your mind ... any thoughts, words, sensations. Focus on these impressions so that they become clearer. Whenever your concentration starts to wander bring it back to this steady beam. You are open and receptive … your channel is clear. Wait, watch, listen inwardly. (Pause for five or ten minutes.)

It is now time to open your eyes. But stay focused on that beam of concentration.

After this exercise go round the group, encouraging each person to describe any impressions they received, no matter how vague or how unlikely they may seem. You can continue the meeting by going round the group again, focusing the power on each person in turn and inviting them to attune to spirit and try to 'pick up' a communicator for someone else within the group. Focusing the power in this way gives the person whose turn it is a boost of energy which will raise their consciousness and make it easier for them to be aware of the spirits.

As a variant, you might try providing each person with pen and paper and asking them to write down any words that come into their minds. An interesting experiment I sometimes try is to give out colouring pencils and ask everyone to draw any spirit communicators of whom they are aware. This does not require any artistic ability and it doesn't matter how rough the drawing is. The mere act of trying to see stimulates the clairvoyant ability.

Keep notes of any interesting information that comes through and, if the communicators cannot be identified by the person for whom they are intended, ask that person to make enquiries among their friends and family. Nothing gives an aspiring medium more confidence than when someone says something like, 'I asked my mother about that man you described called Tom, and she told me that was her grandfather!'

Developing the gift of mediumship can take a long time – months, or even years, depending upon people's inborn potential and the amount of effort they put into it. If, after a few months, you feel you are not making any progress in this direction but you nevertheless enjoy being in the circle, do not feel that attending the group meetings is a waste of time. Perhaps you were not meant to become a medium, but you may find you are developing other, equally valuable, gifts such as healing or the ability to meditate. If the group is helping you to expand your own spirituality in whatever way is best for you, then it is of value and the light you bring will also help everyone else within the group to expand their spiritual awareness.

## CHANNELLING GROUPS

A small, intimate group is an ideal place in which to develop the gift of channelling. The friendship and support the members provide for each other gives much needed encouragement and helps the channeller to build self-confidence. Probably not everyone within the group will find themselves able to let the guides speak through them. For some people, channelling involves making a deep contact with their own higher selves. Others may receive the energy of the higher realms wordlessly and radiate it from their hearts to the rest of the group and, indeed, to everyone with whom they come into contact. It could be argued that this is the highest form of channelling.

Those who feel moved to speak may be too inhibited to open their mouths in public or may fear that they are interrupting the meditation of the other members. This difficulty can be overcome by setting a fixed time for silent meditation, after which the whole group is called back. Then go round the group focusing the power for a few minutes on each person in turn. During this time, the person concerned is encouraged to speak any words that are coming into their mind. Again, pen and paper can be provided for members to write down the words that come to them, should they find it easier to receive information in this way.

It is important that one member of the group always remains detached from the meditation so that they can keep an eye on the others. Have a tape recorder handy to record anything that comes through. Channellers frequently do not recall what they say and, when the tape is played back, may be pleasantly surprised to hear what the guides have said through them.

## HEALING GROUPS

Some of the best groups I have sat in have been healing groups. Healing always calls down a vibrant energy and brings the presence of angels. No special qualifications are needed to run or join such a group – only a loving heart and a sincere desire to be of service to others. You should, however, study how healing works (see Chapter 8).

Distant healing is particularly suited for groups. In all the groups I run, I like to take a few minutes to go round the group asking each person in turn to put forward the names of anyone who is in need of healing at that time. The group then sends healing to all these people, asking that each one be helped in the way that is best for them. I also have a healing book, in which the names of all these people are entered.

The group can also give each other healing as a means of practising. (Remember not to give contact healing if you are tired or unwell.) When everyone has enough experience to feel confident in their ability, friends who need healing can be invited to attend. For anyone in particular need, 'battery healing' can be used. For this, one member of the group gives the healing while the rest also concentrate their power. The effect of this combined energy can be almost enough to lift the patient off the chair! It is certainly very powerful in its results.

I like to end each meeting of all the groups I run with a prayer to gather the healing that has been generated and send it out into the world. You could use or adapt the following.

### PRAYER TO SEND OUT HEALING
We call upon the healing guides and the holy angels of light to bless this sanctuary and to build up the healing energy within

its walls. We ask that the power generated in this group this evening may be taken and used wherever there is pain and suffering. We send this light out to all we know, our families and friends, those we meet in our work and in our leisure. We ask that the light reach out to enfold the whole area where we live. May it travel beyond, to those places in the world where there is war, famine and disease. May it touch all sad and lonely hearts, bringing peace. We ask that the healing angels work with and through us, that we may be channels of healing in our daily lives.

The power of all these groups, whether for meditation or healing, or as a channel of communication with the higher dimension, cannot be over-estimated. The groups help their members to unfold their particular gifts and to develop spiritual understanding and strength. Their blessing spreads beyond the place where they are held. Research has shown that if only 1 or 2 per cent of the inhabitants of an area are meditators, the crime rate in that area drops appreciably. Think what we could achieve if everyone joined with their friends in groups like this!

Each group sends out its own light. I like to think of all those little lights, shining, unknown to each other, and building up into one great flame that will encompass the world in love and healing.

# CHAPTER 11

# Recalling Past Lives

The growing belief in reincarnation in the Western world is another sign of the New Age consciousness that is making itself evident today. When I began my work about twenty-five years ago I was reluctant to broach this subject with sitters, being unsure as to how they would react. These days I find that a great many people are convinced that they have lived before. The information about their past lives that is given to them by the guides is extremely valuable in helping them to understand their present existence, the issues they are dealing with and the purpose for which they came to the earth. But the more I study this fascinating subject, the more I realise what a complicated mechanism underlies it. There are deep mysteries here that we have scarcely begun to unravel.

## FAR MEMORIES

In my Church of England days, I had no thought of reincarnation. Even the speakers in the Spiritualist churches I sometimes attended seldom alluded to it. It was only when I began to explore the beliefs of Buddhism and Hinduism that I began to understand this doctrine, and it immediately rang true to me and helped me to fit together some of the pieces in the puzzling jigsaw of belief I was assembling for myself.

According to Eastern philosophy, we have innumerable lives on earth, during the course of which we experience every type of human condition and every shade of emotion. All these experiences are given to us so that our souls can grow and develop. When we die we return to the spirit world for a period of rest and self-assessment. After a time we come to earth again, bearing within us, at an unconscious level, the memory of all that has gone before. What we are today is the product of all that we have been, felt and experienced in all our past lives. With each new life we learn fresh lessons and our souls progress a little further.

In reincarnation I found the answer to the puzzle for which the Christian church could offer no solution. If God is good, why is the world so unjust? The law of karma, which is part of the teaching of reincarnation, teaches that there is no injustice. In fact, the scales of life are very finely balanced. To put it at its most basic, if you do wrong in one life, you must pay for it in another. For example, a person who committed murder in one life might become a murder victim in another. Someone who squandered great wealth might return as a pauper.

Later, more careful study convinced me that this was an over-simplification. The outworkings of karma are very subtle and beyond our comprehension. Karma can be good as well as bad. The pleasant things that happen in our lives can be seen as compensation for unhappy times in the past. Our gifts and talents may have been acquired in earlier lives. What seems like a stroke of good luck may be a reward for past efforts. Even 'bad' karma should not be seen as a punishment for our misdeeds. Rather, we are put into situations where we are confronted with lessons we failed to learn in the past, so that hopefully we can overcome our weaknesses and handle these situations better.

Karma offers an explanation for the inequalities of life. It explains why some people who have apparently done no wrong in their lives suffer misfortune or hardship. However, the reason for this is not necessarily that the person has done something wrong in a past life for which they are atoning. The suffering may be a test, through which the inner being is perfecting itself. If it sometimes seems that it is the best and most spiritual people who suffer the most, this may be because in the school of life, as in any school, the best and most advanced pupils are given the hardest lessons.

We are all here to learn. Once we grasp this concept, the trials and tribulations of life seem less of a burden. Every experience is an opportunity, if only we can approach it in the light of spiritual understanding. We cannot avoid pain and suffering but we have a choice. Will we become embittered by it or will we use it to gain inner strength and to make us more sympathetic to the sufferings of others? Other people will hurt us but the challenge is to forgive. They, too, are on their spiritual journey. We are bound to fail at times and to make mistakes. That is all part of being human. But we have to forgive ourselves as well and to gain wisdom from these failures.

When I first began to comprehend this philosophy it was on one level a revelation to me. I had fantasies of ancient Egypt and myself as Cleopatra being rowed down the Nile on a barge. But on another level, what I was learning struck a deep chord as though I had simply been reminded of something that inwardly I had always known. As for Cleopatra, more sober reflection convinced me that if I had been around at that time, I would probably have been a galley slave!

But having accepted that I had lived before, I found that past memories came back to me spontaneously in meditation. One of these was of a life in a convent in France, in the early part of the Middle Ages. Time and time again I saw a picture of myself as a young nun. I used to play a small organ and I taught the novices to sing in the choir. That life had its echoes in the present. I was strongly drawn to the church and to the monastic life. Books about nuns had always fascinated me. And I still played the church organ and sang in the choir.

Other memories of that time surfaced. I remembered going with one of the other nuns to the market to buy provisions. I could feel the coarseness of the habit I wore and the cold and discomfort of the long hours spent lying prostrate in front of the altar because of some sin or breach of the rules. I believe that this life ended violently. I have some confused impressions of soldiers entering the convent, pillaging the church, and of myself being slain by a sword.

In another more ancient time I saw myself as a minor priest at the temple of Karnak. Despite my religious role, I lived a worldly life. My job was to teach the young boys in the school attached to the temple. My life ended when I failed in a dangerous initiation. I had no proof that either of these lives were anything but a figment of my imagination, except for one curious event. Some time later I was watching a television programme about Karnak in which the presenter, a woman, was walking through the ruins of the temple. It flashed through my mind, with a burst of anger, 'She shouldn't be there – women weren't allowed in that part of the temple!' Seconds later, the presenter remarked, as she continued her commentary, 'This is an area of the temple where women were not permitted.'

Other memories were triggered off by events in this life or by people I met. When I first met my husband I knew that we had been together before. I didn't know when or where, but there was an instant sense of recognition. Once, when I was introduced to a woman at a church, I instinctively knew that we had been together in France in the seventeenth century, and that we had been cousins and had played together as children. She and I became close friends, and later when we discussed my memory it transpired that she had independently recalled the same life.

Visits to new places also sparked off memories. When I went on holiday to Greece with a girlfriend and we were sight-seeing at the Parthenon, I was overcome with such a deep sense of sadness that I wanted to cry. She asked me what was wrong but I couldn't tell her. That night, we attended a son et lumière presentation. As I sat on the hill opposite the Acropolis, watching the lights and listening to the commentary, it suddenly flashed into my mind that I had been there as a child when the temple had been destroyed. I vividly recalled my anger and distress as even the little trees that grew around the temple were ripped up by the attackers. On checking history books later, I could find no reference to the Parthenon having been destroyed in ancient times, although an earlier temple on the site had suffered this fate, so my memories may have harked back to that very early period. My parents were killed in this attack, and I spent the rest of that life in loneliness. The impressions were so vivid that I do believe it was a genuine memory.

Television programmes brought back quite a few memories. I would see some picture that seemed instantly familiar then later, in my meditation, scenes would arise in my mind. A programme about the Cathars brought back horrific memories – which even now I prefer not to dwell on – of torture and death when, as a heretic (not necessarily a Cathar, I feel, but a member of some persecuted sect in that period) I watched my son being burned at the stake. I myself was imprisoned in a high, round tower, where I eventually died of neglect.

Fascinated by these and other impressions of past lives, I began trying to write them all down. Though the lives were so varied, there did seem to be certain themes running through them: there was religious vocation, as a nun, priestess or member of various kinds of sects; music recurred several times; and in several lives I have been a spiritual teacher, which also seems to be my mission in this life.

In retrospect, I was probably naive to imagine that I could set out my soul's history, like plotting a family tree. Doubtless there were many lives that I could not recall. It should also be borne in mind that some of what we imagine to be past lives may have another explanation: products of the imagination or fantasies based on some forgotten incident in childhood. Some memories may be genetic, inherited from our ancestors. Others may come from spirit communicators who impress their memories on our minds. Alternatively, perhaps we are able to tap into some vast universal pool of memories, what Jung called the collective unconscious. Some people even believe that our lives are not linear, that some part of our consciousness is out of time and we can go back as well as forwards.

All these possibilities – which I do not have space to explore in detail here – make the subject of reincarnation immensely complex and mean that we should not glibly take every 'past-life memory' at face value. There is, however, very strong evidence that reincarnation does take place. One of the greatest pioneers in this field, Dr Ian Stevenson, has collected many cases where children, particularly in India and the East, have given precise details about their former lives and families, and this information has been verified. Moreover, some of these children have exhibited birthmarks which reflect the way in which they died. One boy, for instance, had a round birthmark on his head in precisely the place where he was shot in his previous life.

A fascinating case history is given in Jenny Cockell's book *Yesterday's Children*. The author recalled a life earlier this century in which she had lived in the small Irish town of Malahide. Her abiding memory was of dying in hospital in a state of great anxiety about her eight children whom she was leaving behind. Delving into these memories, and with considerable detective work, Jenny discovered that her name had been Mary Sutton. She was able to contact two of her surviving children. Her son, Sonny, was amazed when she told him about incidents that had occurred in his childhood, and he fully accepted that Jenny was his mother reborn.

## REGRESSION THERAPY

Further evidence for reincarnation is provided through regression therapy. This is a process which involves putting a patient into a state of hypnosis or deep relaxation in order to uncover the root cause of physical or emotional problems, fears or phobias. Often the cause lies in childhood, or even in the prenatal state. But sometimes it is necessary to go even further back, to a past life. Although this idea is rejected by most psychiatrists, some are reluctantly coming round to accept the possibility of past-life recall. What lends validity to the argument is that, in many cases, once patients have gone back in their mind to the origin of the trauma, the fear or anxiety associated with it is released and healing can take place.

One of the most influential therapists in this field is Dr Brian Weiss, whose book *Many Lives, Many Masters* has become a bestseller. Dr Weiss, who had no previous belief in reincarnation, was treating a patient, Catherine, who was suffering from phobias, panic attacks and recurring nightmares. After a year of conventional psychiatric treatment Catherine was showing no improvement so Dr Weiss decided to regress her, using hypnosis. To his surprise, when he instructed her to go back to the time when her symptoms arose, instead of going to childhood, Catherine flipped back four thousand years into an ancient near-Eastern lifetime in which she had been drowned, and then to a number of other lives. Dr Weiss assumed that she was fantasising – but over the weeks her symptoms began to clear up until she was completely better. This impressed him so deeply that he began to investigate past-life therapy. He has subsequently regressed hundreds of patients and has found that they have responded more dramatically by this method than through months of psychiatry.

My own experience of regression took place some years ago. I once again found myself travelling back to a life in France, this time in the eighteenth century. I was a wealthy woman, living in a chateau outside Paris. But my life was not a happy one. I was old and suffered from arthritis. I had no close family and most of my friends had died. As I went deeper into the regression I could recapture the feelings of loneliness and isolation, even while, at the same time, I was conscious of my present personality. I sought consolation for my loneliness in religion, endowing a local convent. I also took an interest in clairvoyants and soothsayers. 'Did you go to see them?' my therapist asked. And I heard my voice replying haughtily, 'They came to me!'

That life felt very real to me. When I was a child in this life I had pictured myself as a grand lady. One of my favourite games was dressing up. I would pull the eiderdown and bed cover off the bed and drape them round me like a long skirt, dragging them around the house, to the annoyance of my mother. I always felt that I should be wearing long, flowing dresses and was uncomfortable in short skirts. And I was very much drawn to France and the French language, in which I did well at school.

## PAST-LIFE READINGS

Though I do not practise regression therapy, the subject of re-incarnation often comes up in the sittings I give. The information the guides give cannot, of course, be verified in the way that facts about deceased relatives or friends can be checked. But it is interesting how often what a sitter is told will strike a chord of recognition. A woman who was told by the guides that she had had a life in India responded, 'I went to India on holiday and I felt completely at home there.' Another woman who enjoyed painting as a hobby was not surprised to be told that she had once been an artist.

The guides do not give this sort of information to satisfy idle curiosity. It is only given when it will help sitters to understand their present life better or give insights into any problems they may be experiencing. Difficulties concerning relationships, for instance, may well be karmic in origin. Most, if not all of the people who are significant in our lives are people we have known before. The way we feel about them and the way we react towards them will be influenced by these previous encounters, which in some cases have left deep wounds in the soul.

Jacky, who was trapped in an unhappy relationship with a violent partner, told me, 'I know I should leave him but I just can't break away.' The guides told her that she had been married to this man in Victorian times, when she had been completely dominated by him. The fear she had felt then was still lodged in her sub-conscious, holding her back. This knowledge gave her the understanding she needed to end the relationship.

Claire was strongly attracted to a married man. 'I know I've known him before,' she confided, 'so we must be meant for each other. But there are so many obstacles in the way. For one thing, he's married.' Gently, her guide explained that although she and the man had been lovers in more than one past life – and this was the reason for the overwhelming attraction they felt for each other – it was not the plan for them to be together this time round. Though this saddened her, it helped her to understand the situation and she decided to stop seeing him.

Lynne wanted to know about the connection between herself and her adopted son, Peter, who was disabled. She wondered why, though it had not been her intention to adopt a disabled child, she had felt compelled to give this particular child a home. She was told that in a past life Peter had been her son but, because of circumstances over which she had no control, she had not been able to give him the love and care he needed. He had been brought back to her now in order that she could show him that love. And in doing that she enabled Peter, who had chosen this difficult incarnation for his own learning process, to fulfil his soul's destiny in this lifetime.

Health is another issue that is frequently raised. Some of our physical weaknesses and illnesses are carried over from the past. For instance, someone who suffers with persistent neck pain may at some time have been hanged. One of the possible causes of anorexia and other eating disorders is starvation in a past life. When a person dies traumatically, through illness, an accident or murder, the memory of that death can be imprinted on the soul and can resurface if it is triggered by emotions in this life.

In my own case, I asked my guides about the bronchial troubles from which I have suffered since I was a child. I was shown a number of lives in which I had died of suffocation or from pneumonia, consumption and other chest complaints. I seem to have made a habit of this, so much so that I have often joked that I caught a chill in the Middle Ages and never quite recovered! Watching the scenes in my mind, I consciously forgave those who had caused my death in the past through violence or cruelty. As I did so the old, deeply held sadness in my soul dissipated, and from that time on my health has improved.

Forgiveness is a major factor in releasing past-life traumas. What causes the trauma to remain locked inside us is not the event itself but the emotion associated with it. Once we are able to forgive whose who have injured us and, when necessary, to forgive ourselves, the emotion is released and healing can take place.

John, a young healer, wanted to know why he carried so much anger and aggression inside him, despite having had a happy childhood within a loving family. The guides told him of a life when he had been imprisoned for a crime he had not committed. After many years confined to a cold, dirty prison cell he had died of a fever, cursing those who had falsely accused him. With this information, he was able to go back to that time in his own meditation and to forgive the perpetrators. As his soul healed, so his healing gift flowered as it never had before.

Many psychics have carried their gifts over from past lives when they were priests, priestesses or magicians. In some cases they abused these gifts and are now making reparation by using them in a spiritual way. Some carry the scars of persecution, having been burned at the stake, tortured or killed in various terrible ways. A lot of sitters have spent lives in monasteries or convents. Where this was a true vocation, such a life may have been an important lesson in the soul's development, giving a deeply felt spirituality and a natural aptitude for prayer and meditation. But it can leave its echo in less happy ways. A person who has lived in an enclosed order may find it hard to relate to other people or to form close attachments.

Angela, who is a Roman Catholic (as are quite a few of my sitters) felt so strongly drawn to the religious life that she was considering entering a convent. The advice she was given by her guide – though, of course, it was only advice and the final choice was left to her – was that convent life felt familiar to her because she had been a nun in the past. In this life, however, she had no need to repeat this lesson and in fact her task was to stay in the world and share her spiritual knowledge with others.

Healers, too, may bring back their gifts from earlier days. They are often drawn to natural medicine and to the use of traditional herbal remedies because they have been skilled in the use of these remedies before. Some souls have come back bearing knowledge of very ancient cultures when man was in tune with the natural world, and their mission is to help in the healing of the earth itself.

## COMING BACK

Some years ago, I had a strange dream. I dreamed that I was with a large number of souls who were preparing to be reborn. These souls were being put onto trains to take them back to earth. Some jumped on board eagerly, impatient to arrive. Others were reluctant. I got into the last compartment of the last train. As the door closed I looked back to some beings for whom I felt infinite love, and said, 'I will never forget you!' I woke up with tears in my eyes.

Whenever I have recounted this dream in talks and workshops, although the idea of souls getting onto trains has provoked laughter, the dream has evoked echoes in my listeners because it does contain a symbolic truth. We come into this world from the spirit world and the memory of that existence remains in our subconscious. This explains the underlying sense of loss and sadness experienced by so many seekers on the spiritual path. I describe it as a spiritual homesickness – a longing for a place that is the soul's true home and to which we will one day return.

Spiritual people, for whom this world is often a hard battle, often say to me, 'I hope this is my last life. I don't want to come back again.' This is a sentiment I share, though I fear that very few of us have reached the end of our earthly lives or we would be saints!

I felt this spiritual homesickness from my earliest years. When I was young I had a sense of being a mature being trapped inside a body that was too small. I resented being treated as a child, being ruled by other people and told what to do. That is, perhaps, the origin of that rebellious streak in me that sometimes surfaced and surprised people who thought I was such a quiet little thing!

I have always believed that my spiritual homesickness was the beginning of my mediumship. Those beings I was leaving behind were the souls who are now my guides. They were the presences I felt as a child and they have remained with me all my life because they are members of my soul group.

We all belong to groups, souls who are bound together by close spiritual ties that are stronger than those of the earthly family. At any time, some of the group will be on earth while others are existing in various spiritual dimensions. Sometimes we incarnate together into the same family or we may meet as friends, lovers or marriage partners. In the time between lives we are reunited. I have known my guides over many lifetimes. Perhaps there have been times when they have been on earth and I have watched over them!

This raises the question of how often we come back to earth. As a medium, this is obviously an important concern for me. I am often asked, 'How can you talk to spirits if they have reincarnated?' I do not claim to be able to give a definitive answer to this question. Some of the children interviewed by Dr Stevenson had apparently been reincarnated very soon after their death. A child who dies young may return quickly because the soul has been deprived of the experience of living on earth. On the other hand, some of the children who are handicapped or who suffer disease are most beautiful, advanced souls. In their case, they may have needed to come only for a short time, perhaps not so much for themselves but to teach the lessons of love and compassion to those around them. These children will have no need to re-incarnate for many years, if at all. They grow to maturity in the spirit world and may remain close to their families, watching over them.

As far as I can understand it, the amount of time that passes between lives depends entirely on the individual, but may be hundreds of years in earthly terms. I have never, when seeking to contact a particular spirit on behalf of a sitter, been told, 'That person is not here, he has reincarnated.' Certainly, spirit communicators usually say that they were met on their arrival in that world by a husband, parent, grandparent or someone they loved, who is there waiting for them.

## REMEMBERING PAST LIVES

Past-life memories can surface spontaneously in meditation. If this doesn't happen for you, it is advisable not to force the issue by getting a friend to try to hypnotise you. This may bring up traumatic memories and disturbing emotions. Should you feel prompted to explore this issue, or should you have problems in your life that you feel may have their roots in an earlier incarnation, seek out a qualified regression therapist who will be able to help you to uncover your memories in a secure, protected environment.

The following guided visualisation is not meant to take you into a deep regression. It is designed to lead you gently into a slightly altered state of consciousness where you can safely explore impressions of past lives without becoming emotionally involved. This exercise works well in a group, with the leader of the group reading the script. This should be done very slowly, with long pauses where marked. The leader should watch to ensure that no one is becoming distressed or uncomfortable. In the unlikely event that this should happen, repeat the sentences stressing that they are watching the events as spectators and will not become emotionally involved in any scene they witness. Then talk the distressed person gently back into the present.

Alternatively, the exercise can be carried out with a partner who reads the script, or you can tape record it and play it back for yourself. You should be lying down or sitting in a comfortable chair which supports your head. Start with the Progressive Relaxation exercise then continue as follows.

## A PAST-LIFE VISUALISATION

You are walking along by the bank of a river. It is summertime
... the breeze is warm ... the birds are singing. You feel the sun
shining down on your head, making patterns of light on the
grass at your feet. On your left is a wood. See the green of the
trees ... listen to the wind rustling the branches. You feel safe
and contented and very, very relaxed.

On your right-hand side is a wide river. The water is a deep,
deep blue ... it is very still. You notice on your side of the bank
a little boat, tied up by a length of string to a wooden post.
Climb into the boat and untie it. The timbers creak as you sit
down but you feel safe. You know you can trust the boat to take
you where you want to go. And now the boat starts drifting,
slowly, slowly ... drifting across the river, borne by the breeze.
Relax and enjoy the gentle rocking motion. Dangle your hand
in the water. Feel how cool it is. See the little fish darting to and
fro beneath you.

The boat is carrying you to the opposite bank of the river.
You are reaching the bank now. The boat stops by an old tree.
Climb out of the boat and tie it with the rope to the tree. Walk
along the river bank. You now come to an old brick wall. Go up
to the wall ... touch the ivy that grows over it. There is a door
in this wall. It is made of iron and is very ancient ... the hinges
are rusty and there is a handle. Take the handle with both your
hands and turn it. Push open the door and step through it.
When you reach the other side of the door you will be in
another life. You will recall this life but you will not become
emotionally involved. You will not be frightened or upset by
anything you see.

Look around you. What do you see? Are you in the countryside or are there buildings around? What country is it? Are you
alone or with other people? What year is it? Look down at
yourself ... are you a man or a woman? How old are you? What
colour is your skin? What are you wearing? What are you doing?
How do you feel about this lifetime? Is it a good life or a

difficult life? (Pause for about five minutes.)

Now I want you to go to some time in that life when you were happy. What is going on? What are you doing? How old are you now? What are you feeling? Is there anyone with you? You are watching this scene but you are not emotionally involved … you are just a spectator. All this happened in another time. This person is another aspect of you. Your higher self is bringing back these memories to give you insights into your life today. Watch what you are seeing. You are quite safe and relaxed. Let the pictures come into your mind. I will leave you for a few minutes to explore these memories. (Pause for ten or fifteen minutes.)

I am now going to bring you back … but before I do so, I want you to release any bad memories of that life. If you feel any pain associated with that time, any regrets, any guilt, consciously let it go now. If anyone in that life hurt or injured you in any way, send them forgiveness. Let any negative emotions float away. They belong to another lifetime, another part of your being. You do not need them now.

It is time to leave that scene behind. Turn and walk away. Come back through the door in the wall … step through it … close it behind you. The boat is waiting for you. Untie it and step into it. Sit down and let it carry you back across the river, feeling the gentle motion as it moves across the water. Now you have arrived at the other side of the river. Step out of the boat onto the bank. Walk back along the path by the woods. You are now coming back into your everyday consciousness. Take a few deep breaths. Be aware of your body … stretch your arms and legs … feel the chair you are sitting on. When you open your eyes you will be wide awake and very refreshed. Open your eyes now. You are wide awake.

# CHAPTER 12

# The Divine Light Within

The other day I came across an old photograph of my father in his shop, surrounded by rolls of wallpaper and tins of paint. My mind went back to the days when I used to help him there, when I would stand in the shop doorway gazing, fascinated, at the Spiritualist church next door.

Looking back over the years that have rolled by since then, I am aware of how the course of my life has been guided and gently steered, and how even the difficulties have been part of the plan that has led me to where I am today. Had it not been for the psychic experiences that caused such problems in my childhood I would not have had the courage and determination to strike out on a different path. I would never have understood my inborn gift or started on the spiritual search that has given my life meaning and fulfilment.

Had I not moved to Wimbledon when I got married I would never have discovered the Spiritualist church there, where I met so many excellent mediums and was invited to join my first development group. Wimbledon was also the beginning of my writing career, when I wrote about those mediums in books designed to explain Spiritualism and life after death to those who were, as I once was, full of curiosity but a little nervous of what it was all about.

And so it has been throughout my life. Whatever has happened to me, it has been for a purpose, even if the purpose was not clear at the time. Always I have been brought into contact with the right people – friends and teachers – who have helped and inspired me. And whenever I have been feeling discouraged or seemed to be losing my way those invisible friends, my spiritual family, have gently picked me up, dusted me down and put my feet on the right road once more.

## TIMES OF CHANGE

When I think back over the last few decades I am conscious of the great changes that have taken place in so many different ways, some positive, some negative. Disasters, both natural and man-made, seem to be more prevalent. Ever-worsening pollution threatens the environment. Global warming is an internationally acknowledged problem. The destruction of the rainforests and the depletion of the ozone layer have repercussions not only for the parts of the earth directly affected but for the whole planet. Storms and freak weather conditions are causing devastation in many countries. Even in Britain the climate is changing. The seasons are no longer so predictable and flooding is becoming more and more of a problem.

Wars rage in many parts of the world, and elsewhere unrest simmers just below the surface, poised to erupt. Vicious crimes such as mugging are on the increase. The recently coined expression 'road-rage' is a worrying indication of how common acts of violence are becoming in our society. We now have a situation where, in many areas, vulnerable people are afraid to walk the streets at night or to travel on public transport alone. Parents are fearful for their children.

These alarming factors are sometimes referred to as signs that the world is approaching a time of dramatic upheaval. Prophets and channellers who predicted a cataclysm for the year 2000 have been proved wrong, but some believe that the time cannot be far away. The prophecies of doom include a nuclear disaster, either deliberate or accidental, massive earthquakes and a shift in the earth's axis with consequences that would wipe out a large per-centage of the world's population. Others more optimistically predict that, although there will be traumatic events, these will bring about a sudden evolution in the consciousness of mankind, ushering in a new age of peace and brotherhood.

Who can say which of these predictions, if any, are right? Perhaps it is as well that we do not know what lies around the corner. It may be that changes will come gradually rather than in one world-wide catastrophe. And there are hopeful indications that the changes may indeed be for the better. Despite all the violence and negativity, a gentler, more caring attitude is beginning to make itself felt today. Wherever there is war, famine or flood, aid agencies work to bring help to the victims. Every disaster brings in response large sums of money in donations from ordinary men and women who are moved by compassion. Organisations such as Greenpeace campaign to halt the destruction of the environment. Though governments and industry lag behind, once again it is ordinary people everywhere who support the campaigners, driven by a growing sense of urgency to save the world before it is irreparably damaged.

In the field of science, a quiet revolution is taking place. While traditional scientists remain entrenched in a mechanistic world view, their younger colleagues are exploring other avenues, seeking new ways of understanding the world that acknowledge the spiritual dimension. One of the most notable pioneers is James Lovelock whose Gaia hypothesis views the earth as a sentient being and sees all life as interconnected. No longer does man seem to be alone in the universe. Thirty years ago no serious scientist would have admitted the possibility of there being intelligent life forms anywhere in space. Now, millions of dollars are spent every year on research projects to seek for signals that may be coming in from some distant part of the galaxy – though science is a long way from taking note of the 'channellings' from extraterrestrials!

Within medicine there have also been significant developments. After so many years of being on the fringes and regarded as 'cranky', all forms of healing and complementary medicine are now accepted as almost mainstream. Thousands of people, disillusioned with drugs, are recognising the advantages of these gentle and non-invasive forms of treatment that take account of the spirit as well as the body.

Nowhere is the change more apparent than in the field of the psychic and the spiritual. The last two or three decades have seen an explosion of interest in all aspects of the supernatural.

Channelling, mediumship, tarot, astrology, past-life regression, angels and feng shui are just a few of the subjects that have been popularised. Never has such a great proliferation of psychic books been published. Every bookshop now has its mind/body/spirit section, to say nothing of the information circulating on the internet.

Workshops, seminars and courses are springing up everywhere. Even colleges and universities are responding to this trend. My local evening institute now offers courses in aromatherapy and feng shui, which would certainly not have formed part of the curriculum twenty or thirty years ago.

This public enthusiasm, of course, has its down side. Self-appointed teachers and gurus are jumping onto the psychic band-wagon. Great care and discrimination is necessary to assess what is available, and the gullible can easily be exploited. But it is also immensely exciting that knowledge that was once the preserve of occult societies is now freely available to all.

The media, that barometer of public opinion, reflects this trend. A few years ago psychic subjects, if they were featured at all, were regarded as light entertainment at best, and at worst were ridiculed and debased. Now they are often given serious coverage in newspapers and magazines and on television. As these matters are brought out into the open more and more there is a snowball effect. People are starting to talk more about their beliefs and experiences with less fear of being laughed at or thought peculiar. Celebrities air their views in public, encouraging their readers and listeners to think that if the trendy and famous can admit to seeing an astrologer or a medium or having an out-of-the-body experience, then it must be all right for everyone else to talk about such things!

The change is most clearly seen in the new generation. Many of the children born within the last ten or fifteen years have a special quality of spirituality. They have a natural, unquestioning sense of the spirit within and an easy acceptance of the spirit world, unmarred by fear. Many parents tell me things their children have said which have astonished them. Jane told me that her little son was only three when his grandfather died, but he sees him sitting on the end of his bed and he chats away to him quite happily.

Angela was amazed by the little Romanian girl, Claudia, who had been adopted by a couple she knew well. 'When mummy has a pain in her shoulders,' Claudia told Angela, 'I just put my hands on her shoulders and I get tingles in my fingers. I ask gentle Jesus to take the pain away and then the tingling stops and I go out and play.' And she asked Angela, 'Is that what you do when you give healing?'

Joan wrote to me about her granddaughter Hannah.

When Hannah was about two and a half years old she told her mother that there were always people around her bed at night. When she came to stay with me I asked her if there were people around her bed at my house and she replied, 'Of course. They are my guides.'

And Sue told me about her daughter Stephanie, who showed a remarkable insight into the different dimensions of the astral world when they went out together on a drive in the country.

Stephanie was looking up at the clouds. She said, 'That's the entrance to heaven. If you go up the stairs to the golden light, you will be back with God. If you have murdered someone or done something wrong, then you fall into the red light. Sometimes there is a trampoline and you can bounce back up'.

I couldn't have put it better myself!

## THE CHANGING FACE OF MEDIUMSHIP

When I began my work as a medium, Doris Stokes was at the height of her popularity. With her publicity meetings in theatres and halls and her bestselling books she did much to change the public's attitude to Spiritualism and mediums. Doris Collins was another very well-known medium at that time, and medium and author Stephen O'Brien also reached hundreds of people through his nationwide tours, as he still does today.

The publicity generated by these meetings has caused many people, including those who would never go inside a Spiritualist church, to take a closer look at the subject of life after death. The investigations into near-death experiences that have been carried out by doctors and scientists, and which have been published in many popular books, have also opened people's minds to the possibility of an existence beyond the grave.

All these things have helped to make my work easier. I no longer feel that I am fighting against a tide of scepticism and ridicule. There is an element of the public that still regards mediums as dotty old ladies sitting in dark rooms calling up the dead, which is how my family had viewed poor Aunt Flo. Some of my sitters who have never been to see a medium before may have this image at the back of their minds, although they are too polite to say so, but most, even if they are a little nervous, don't seriously expect me to bring out the seance table and plunge the room into darkness.

People in general are becoming more psychically aware. Their inner senses are stirring even if they do not know that this is happening. Nearly everyone I talk to admits to having had some sort of psychic experience. They may not understand this experience, they may even have been frightened by it, but they are convinced that there is something beyond the material. If they have lost someone close it is very likely that they have already sensed that person's presence for themselves. Perhaps they have doubts, wondering if what they felt was just their imagination. But underneath those doubts is an instinctive knowing. As one woman said to me, 'I know my husband is there really. I just need you to tell me that I know!'

Because of this growing awareness, the role of the medium has changed. In the past, mediums viewed their task primarily as bringing through spirit loved ones, family and friends, in a way that gave convincing evidence of life after death. There is, of course, still a place for this type of mediumship. In fact, I regard it as a large and vital part of my work. Someone who has been bereaved and who finds it hard to accept the existence of a spiritual dimension needs this kind of personal evidence in order to believe. To provide this, the medium must be able to communicate clearly with the spirits, to provide relevant factual information which the sitter knows could not have been obtained in any other way save from the one in the spirit world. When a bereaved person receives this information and as a result is able to say, 'Now I am sure that life goes on,' the comfort and relief felt is immense.

But, as I mentioned earlier, an increasingly large number of the people who consult mediums are not particularly concerned with this evidence or even, in many cases, with contact with particular individuals among their families in the spirit world. They are more concerned with getting in touch with their guides, either for help with problems in their lives or to find ways of developing their own spiritual awareness. Many are seeking healing, not only physically but at a deep soul level. In order to meet all these different needs I have to be very closely attuned to my own guides. Only then can I be flexible enough to act as a channel of communication on whatever level is most appropriate for each individual.

## HEALING OTHERS, HEALING OURSELVES

With this growing psychic awareness comes a need to find a purpose in life, to do something of value in the world. For when the spirit has awoken we feel compassion stirring within us. We feel we can no longer sit back and do nothing in a world where there is so much pain and suffering.

People often say to me, 'I want to do something but I don't

know what.' The first thing we have to do is work on ourselves. We have to look at ourselves with complete honesty, confront our fears and release outmoded habits, beliefs and thought patterns. This is a difficult task. Undertaking it may bring about a crisis in our lives as we are forced to face up to our shadow side, all that is dark in ourselves. But once we have, the way opens up and we are shown where we can indeed contribute something of value.

There are so many avenues of service. Some people are drawn to various forms of medicine or therapy. Others may find their purpose in helping the poor and homeless or supporting organisations that work for the environment or animal welfare. All these are fundamentally forms of healing. Healing is simply the power of love in action. When we show love and kindness to others, in whatever way, we are giving out healing energy. We are playing our part, however small it may be, in the healing of the world.

But the root meaning of healing is making whole, and we cannot heal others unless we are whole in ourselves. We are in this world to give but we are also here to receive. We learn through our pain and suffering but we also learn through joy and happiness, as students of karma are always telling us. This is all part of finding that essential balance. Life was meant to be joyous and needs to be lived and experienced on every level.

This point came home to me very clearly in a story I was told by a medium called Maggie, who was still recovering from a stroke and a brain haemorrhage. She had been rushed into hospital, where her anxious sons had been told that she was unlikely to survive and that, if she did, she would be an imbecile. But the universe had other plans.

Maggie told me of her near-death experience in which she met her father and her sister.

I saw a beautiful white light and in that light was a figure I instinctively recognised. I knew it was Jesus. It was wonderful! He was talking to me and comforting me.

'Do you want to stay?' he asked.

'Of course I do,' I said. It was beautiful there and I'd had enough of the pain and couldn't take any more.

'Are you sure?' he asked. And I felt that he was not ready to accept me yet. There was something I had to do on earth though I didn't know what it was.

'It's your choice,' the voice said.

I made up my mind. 'I'm going back,' I said. 'I want to finish whatever I came to do so that you'll accept me gladly.'

As I walked away I felt as if I was going towards the edge of a cliff.

'Come back for a moment,' the voice said. 'I will tell you what you have to do.'

What he said was a complete surprise. 'When you go home, please find happiness. We don't want miserable people up here.'

Maggie woke up with a shock, back in her body. She was in severe pain. The stroke had paralysed the whole of her right side. Two days later she had an operation on her brain. A long period of recuperation began. She had to learn to walk and to talk again. Now, six years later, she has not fully recovered, but she does not regret her decision and, despite everything, feels she is on her way to discovering the happiness she came back to find.

We are all sons and daughters of God and in this vast spiritual family every soul is of value. We are not worth more than anyone else, but we are not worth less.

## WHAT I BELIEVE

A while ago I was asked by a sitter whether I believed in God. To me, it is self-evident that there is a God. I couldn't be aware of the spirit world and its many dimensions without believing that there is, above it all, a supreme being guiding and directing the whole universe. When I was young I had a picture of God as an old man with a white beard sitting on a cloud, surrounded by angels playing harps. This is the picture most of us were given as children and it was presumably what my sitter had in mind. Of course, I no longer see God in these terms. To me, God is the power behind all creation, the source of all love, light and energy. He created the universe out of His own being and there is something of His essence in every atom.

'What about Jesus?' my sitter asked.

To answer this question I had to explain how my beliefs have evolved since that day in my teens when, prompted by a half-understood stirring of the soul, I first visited the Anglican church near where I lived. I never felt at ease with the teachings of Christianity. I could not accept that Jesus died on the cross so that man might be saved. I questioned how a God who, supposedly, loved all his children could demand such a sacrifice.

As I studied Christian theology I realised that we really know very little of the historical Jesus. The Bible was not written until many years after his death, by men whose understanding of his teaching was limited by the age and culture in which they lived. Since then it has been edited, translated and manipulated by theologians who have all had their own particular doctrinal axe to grind. The history of the Church throughout the centuries has been marred by hypocrisy, repression and persecution, which has made a mockery of the teaching of the master who came to bring love and peace. Yet I could never reject Jesus himself. However much I doubted intellectually, whenever I prayed to Jesus I felt a response in my heart and knew that my prayers were being heard by an infinitely loving being.

When I started to attend Spiritualist churches I found that there is within Spiritualism a division where Christianity is concerned. Some Spiritualists are adamant that their movement should be set apart from all creeds, honouring every man's beliefs but tied to none. To a large extent I agree with this. All religions enshrine elements of the truth, but the ultimate truth is too far beyond our understanding to be the preserve of any one religion.

But Christian Spiritualists look to Jesus as their spiritual master. Some of them embrace the teachings of the Christian Church in their entirety, but the majority have a less orthodox interpretation. They distinguish between Jesus and Christ. Christ is seen as a universal being emanating from God and set by God over the whole earth. All the great masters who have come to this world to teach have been inspired by this cosmic Christ. Jesus was a pure soul who came as a vehicle for the Christ, a task for which, some believe, he was prepared by many lifetimes.

I do not accept that Jesus took our sins upon himself. We have to work out our own salvation. But Jesus showed us the way of love. The Christ spirit, which he embodied to a unique degree, is present within each one of us. It is the divine spark, the Jewel in the Lotus, the point at which we connect with God. This interpretation, which has been given by many teachers from the spirit world, is one that resonates with me. The Jesus to whom I prayed as a child I still pray to, but I visualise not a man who walked the earth two thousand years ago but a great master who is still active today in the spiritual dimension and who is accessible to all who call upon him.

This, however, is my personal belief. In the end we all have to find our own truth in our hearts. And our beliefs do not have to be set in stone. As our consciousness expands so we modify our beliefs, and concepts which, perhaps, we once rejected come to form part of our enlarged understanding. This is a never-ending process. Even when we pass beyond death we will be only one small step further along the path of discovery, with so much still to learn.

But to find our truth, we have to touch the spirit within. Because deep inside us, in the divine spark, the Christ consciousness, call it what you will, there resides all knowledge and all wisdom. Human beings, in their materialism, have forgotten this and have lost their way. The purpose of life is to reconnect with our divine origins, to find the light within and direct it out into the world.

CHANNELLING THE LIGHT
This meditation is based upon the symbol of the six-pointed star, a powerful symbol of wholeness and healing.

Stand up straight with your spine erect and your feet slightly apart so that you are balanced. Ground and centre yourself. Breathe in and as you do so raise your arms slowly above your head. Visualise a golden light coming down from above your head and flowing all around you. Breathe out and slowly lower your arms, bringing your hands together, a few inches apart, over your heart centre. See a gold six-pointed star at your heart centre and feel the light focusing on the star and pouring through the star into your heart.

Make the affirmation: 'I am a channel for the light. I breathe in the light. My whole being is filled with radiant energy.'

As you do so, feel the energy between your hands and breathe it in until you are strong and energised. Then, on the out-breath, open your arms wide and visualise the star becoming bigger and brighter. Watch it expanding as the light and love streams out from your heart. Sense the presence of your guides and angels working with you. Make the affirmation: 'I join with all beings of light to send love, light and peace into the world.'

When you feel the flow stop, fold your hands once more over your heart centre. Rest for a few minutes then close the chakras in the usual way.

Try to do this exercise every morning and evening. If the weather is suitable, it can be performed outdoors or in front of an open window, where you can breathe in the sunlight. Carried out regularly, this meditation will help you to make and then to hold the connection both with your guides and with your own divine self. Use it to guide and strengthen you on your journey. And may joy and peace go with you.

# Appendix

The largest Spiritualist organisation in Britain is the Spiritualists National Union. This has its headquarters at Stansted in Essex, in the beautiful Jacobean-style manor house bequeathed to it in the 1960s by the writer Arthur Findlay. Stansted Hall is one of the first places you should go to if you are interested in mediumship. It offers a variety of courses in mediumship and healing given by some of the country's leading exponents.

In London there are a number of different and completely independent bodies. The largest of these, the Spiritualist Association of Great Britain, based in Belgrave Square, offers lectures, workshops, healing and demonstrations of clairvoyance. Similar facilities are provided by the Greater World Christian Spiritualist Association, situated near the Post Office Tower. The College of Psychic Studies in Kensington, though not a Spiritualism organisation, provides sittings with mediums, healing and workshops and lectures on a wide range of subjects. In addition, the Institute of Spiritualist Mediums, to which I belong, which is based mainly in London and Essex, exists to promote a high standard of mediumship and to train mediums through lectures, workshops and residential courses.

The principal organisation for healers is the National Federation of Spiritual Healers. This is completely non-denominational; the word 'spiritual' in the title refers to that quality of spirituality implicit in the healing process. The training course provided by the NFSH is quite long and demanding, but at the end of it you will be well qualified and thoroughly versed in your subject. There are other organisations, such as the Spiritualists National Union, which also offer good qualifications.

# Further Reading

Alberdi, Lita de, *Channelling*, Piatkus, 1998

Angelo, Jack, *Your Healing Power*, Piatkus, 1998

Aron, Elaine N:, *The Highly Sensitive Person*, Thorsons, 1999

Brennen, Barbara Ann, *Hands of Light*, Bantam Books, 1988

Cockell, Jenny, *Yesterday's Children*, Piatkus, 1993

Edward, John, *One Last Time*, Piatkus, 1998

Fenwick, Peter and Elizabeth, *Past Lives*, Headline, 1999

Fontana, David, *Meditation: an introductory guide*, Element, 1999

Hall, Judy, *Deja Who?*, Findhorn Press, 1998

Herzberg, Eileen Inge, *Spiritual Healing: a patient's guide*, The C.W. Daniel Co. Ltd, 1988

Macbeth, Jessica, *Moon Over Water*, Gateway Books, 1990

Neate, Tony, *Channelling for Everyone*, Piatkus, 1997

Northage, Ivy, *Light of the World*, Spiritualist Association of Great Britain, 1999

O'Brien, Stephen, *Visions of Another World*, Voices Books, revised edition 2000

Ozaniec, Naomi, *The Elements of the Chakras*, Element Books, 1990

Swarte, Lyn de, *Principles of Spiritualism*, Thorsons, 1999

Stevenson, Ian, *Children Who Remember Previous Lives*, University Press of Virginia, 1987

Weiss, Brian, *Many Lives, Many Masters*, Piatkus, 1994

White Eagle, *Walking With the Angels*, White Eagle Publishing Trust, 1998

White, Ruth, *Working With Your Chakras*, Piatkus, 1993

Williamson, Linda, *Contacting the Spirit World*, Piatkus, 1996

Williamson, Linda, *Children and the Spirit World*, Piatkus, 1997

# *Useful Addresses*

**Australia**
International Council of Spiritualists
PO Box 123, Wandin
Victoria 3139

**New Zealand**
Christian Spiritualist Church of the Golden Light
25 New North Road
Auckland

Spiritualist Alliance (Auckland) Inc.
PO Box 9477
120 Carlton Gore Road
Newmarket, Auckland 1

**South Africa**
Center of Spiritual Studies
PO Box 12234
Moffat Place
Port Elizabeth 6002

**UK**
College of Healing
Runnings Park
Croft Bank
West Malvern
Worcs. WR14 4DU

College of Psychic Studies
16 Queensberry Place
London SW7 2EB

Greater World Christian Spiritualist Association
3–5 Conway Street
London W1P 5HA

Institute of Spiritualist Mediums
121 Churchend Road
Runwell, Wickford
Essex SS11 7DN

International Flower Essence Repertoire
The Living Tree
Milland, Liphook
Hampshire GU30 7JS

International Spiritualist Federation
11a Linkside, Woodside Park
London N12 7LE

National Federation of Spiritual Healers
Old Manor Farm Studio
Church Street
Sunbury-on-Thames
Middlesex TW16 6RG
Helpline: 0891 616080

*Psychic News*
Clock Cottage
Stansted Hall, Stansted
Essex CM24 8UD

*Psychic World*
22 Kingsley Avenue
Southall
Middlesex UB1 2NA

School of Channelling
Runnings Park, Croft Bank
West Malvern
Worcs. WR14 4DU

Spiritualist Association of Great Britain
33 Belgrave Square
London SW1X 8QB

Spiritualists National Union
Stansted Hall, Stansted
Essex CM24 8UD

White Eagle Lodge
New Lands, Brewells Lane
Liss, Hampshire GU33 7HY

**USA**
American Federation of Spiritualist Churches Inc.
145 Herring Pond Road
Buzzards Bay, MA 02532

National Spiritualist Association of Churches
c/o Rev. S.L. Snowman
PO Box 217, Lily Dale
New York, NY 14752

*Other titles of interest also published by Rider …*

## SOUL ENERGY

How to Heal Yourself and Feel Full of Life

Carmel Greenwood

We can all become free spirits with love and joy in our hearts, explains Carmel Greenwood, by being restored to our natural state of purity. In *Soul Energy*, she offers a set of tools that can be used on all levels – physical, mental, emotional and spiritual – to bring ourselves back to our own place of integrity and truth. In this way, we will have more fun, feel full of vitality and our natural creativity will appear.

- Identify your own strengths and weaknesses
- Expand your limits
- Improve your relationships with yourself and others
- Embrace change with enthusiasm

By learning about the power points of your body (your chakras) – and how to balance them – you can rediscover who you truly are: a unique and loving individual who enjoys to the full each adventure that life may bring.

'Soul Energy is a superb book about enjoying the highs of life and emerging triumphant from the lows.'   Lillian Too

**SACRED SPACE**

Enhancing the Energy of Your Home & Office

Denise Linn

*'Our homes are mirrors of ourselves. Through them
we can interface with the universe.'*

Everything in the universe is composed of constantly changing
energy, including our homes and their contents. By clearing and
enhancing this energy, we can turn our living spaces not only into
sanctuaries but also into places that radiate positive energy for the
benefit of others.

In this fascinating and unusual book, international lecturer and
healer Denise Linn shows how we can infuse our homes with a
sense of cosmic order so they become nurturing centres of
strength and health. Drawing on her Cherokee Indian heritage, as
well as the knowledge she has personally collected from the native
traditions around the world, Denise offers simple yet effective
techniques including the use of

- Feng Shui
- Spirit Smoke
- Purifying Fire
- Mystic Sound
- The Way of the Shaman

to help us create a sacred space wherever we make our home.

**Soul Energy** by Carmel Greenwood        £9.99
**Sacred Space** by Denise Linn        £7.99

ALL RIDER BOOKS ARE AVAILABLE THROUGH MAIL ORDER OR FROM YOUR LOCAL BOOKSHOP.

PAYMENT MAY BE MADE USING ACCESS, VISA, MASTER-CARD, DINERS CLUB, SWITCH AND AMEX, OR CHEQUE, EUROCHEQUE AND POSTAL ORDER (STERLING ONLY).

EXPIRY DATE ................................. SWITCH ISSUE NO.

SIGNATURE ................................................................................

PLEASE ALLOW £2.50 FOR POST AND PACKING FOR THE FIRST BOOK AND £1.00 PER BOOK THEREAFTER.

ORDER TOTAL: £......................................... (INCLUDING P&P)

ALL ORDERS TO:
RIDER BOOKS, BOOKS BY POST, TBS LIMITED, THE BOOK SERVICE, COLCHESTER ROAD, FRATING GREEN, COLCHESTER, ESSEX, CO7 7DW, UK.

TELEPHONE: (01206) 256 000
FAX:          (01206) 255 914

NAME ...........................................................................................

ADDRESS .....................................................................................

...................................................................................................

Please allow 28 days for delivery. Please tick box if you do not wish to receive any additional information. ☐
Prices and availability subject to change without notice.